W9-BZL-313

THE BEDFORD SERIES IN HISTORY AND CULTURE

# Crosscurrents in the Black Atlantic, 1770–1965

## A Brief History with Documents

Related Titles in
# THE BEDFORD SERIES IN HISTORY AND CULTURE
*Advisory Editors*: Lynn Hunt, *University of California, Los Angeles*
David W. Blight, *Yale University*
Bonnie G. Smith, *Rutgers University*
Natalie Zemon Davis, *Princeton University*
Ernest R. May, *Harvard University*

---

THE BEDFORD SERIES IN HISTORY AND CULTURE

# Crosscurrents in the Black Atlantic, 1770–1965

## A Brief History with Documents

## David Northrup
*Boston College*

BEDFORD/ST. MARTIN'S     Boston  ♦  New York

*For Bedford/St. Martin's*

*Publisher for History:* Mary V. Dougherty
*Director of Development for History:* Jane Knetzger
*Developmental Editor:* Betty Slack
*Editorial Assistant:* Laurel Damashek
*Senior Production Supervisor:* Joe Ford
*Production Associates:* Maureen O'Neill, Sarah Ulicny
*Executive Marketing Manager:* Jenna Bookin Barry
*Project Management:* Books By Design, Inc.
*Index:* Books By Design, Inc.
*Cover Design:* Liz Tardiff
*Cover Art: Atlantic Ocean* by Samuel Goodrich. From *A Universal Illustrated Atlas, Exhibiting a Geographical, Statistical and Historical View of the World,* 1841. Photo courtesy of Murray Hudson Books and Maps, Halls, Tennessee, and the Cartographic Research Laboratory, Department of Geography, University of Alabama.
*Composition:* Stratford/TexTech
*Printing and Binding:* RR Donnelley & Sons Company

*President:* Joan E. Feinberg
*Editorial Director:* Denise B. Wydra
*Director of Marketing:* Karen Melton Soeltz
*Director of Editing, Design, and Production:* Marcia Cohen
*Manager, Publishing Services:* Emily Berleth

Library of Congress Control Number: 2007920786

2  1  0  9  8  7
f  e  d  c  b  a

*For information, write:* Bedford/St. Martin's, 75 Arlington Street, Boston, MA 02116 (617-399-4000)

ISBN-10: 0-312-44244-0
ISBN-13: 978-0-312-44244-6

*Acknowledgments*

Acknowledgments and copyrights are continued at the back of the book on page 173, which constitutes an extension of the copyright page.

# Foreword

The Bedford Series in History and Culture is designed so that readers can study the past as historians do.

The historian's first task is finding the evidence. Documents, letters, memoirs, interviews, pictures, movies, novels, or poems can provide facts and clues. Then the historian questions and compares the sources. There is more to do than in a courtroom, for hearsay evidence is welcome, and the historian is usually looking for answers beyond act and motive. Different views of an event may be as important as a single verdict. How a story is told may yield as much information as what it says.

Along the way the historian seeks help from other historians and perhaps from specialists in other disciplines. Finally, it is time to write, to decide on an interpretation and how to arrange the evidence for readers.

Each book in this series contains an important historical document or group of documents, each document a witness from the past and open to interpretation in different ways. The documents are combined with some element of historical narrative—an introduction or a biographical essay, for example—that provides students with an analysis of the primary source material and important background information about the world in which it was produced.

Each book in the series focuses on a specific topic within a specific historical period. Each provides a basis for lively thought and discussion about several aspects of the topic and the historian's role. Each is short enough (and inexpensive enough) to be a reasonable one-week assignment in a college course. Whether as classroom or personal reading, each book in the series provides firsthand experience of the challenge— and fun—of discovering, recreating, and interpreting the past.

Lynn Hunt
David W. Blight
Bonnie G. Smith
Natalie Zemon Davis
Ernest R. May

# Preface

This book describes and documents the interactions of black individuals and communities around the Atlantic from the mid-eighteenth century to the mid-twentieth century. It shows how Africans and those of African ancestry in the diaspora created by the Atlantic slave trade were reestablishing connections with one another and were rethinking their common ancestry and problems. These interactions included (but were not confined to) African American contacts with Africa and Europe; West Indian contacts with the United States, Europe, and Africa; and African contacts with Europe and the United States. This volume includes selections from individuals who are well-known and others who are less so, but its uniqueness and utility lie in showing how the divided communities around the Atlantic struggled to overcome geographical and cultural separations and build a broad coalition against discrimination and exploitation.

*Crosscurrents in the Black Atlantic, 1770–1965* will be useful for instructors of courses on American history and African American history who wish to expand their coverage of the larger world of contacts outside the territorial boundaries of the United States and for instructors of courses in world history who wish to include greater coverage of black people. The book is especially well suited for use in newer courses in Atlantic history and the black diaspora that emphasize the interactive nature of the Atlantic world for all its neighboring peoples. The examples of assertive black leadership and intellectual vitality presented in this volume serve as a useful complement to coverage of the Atlantic slave trade that inevitably presents a picture of black people as degraded victims. The multiple sources and directions of black contacts around the Atlantic in this volume also provide an intriguing contrast to the one-way passage from Africa to the Americas in the slave-trade era.

Neither a history of all aspects of black life nor an account of the African diaspora, *Crosscurrents in the Black Atlantic* is unique in that it

brings together in a single volume the physical and intellectual interactions of black people around the Atlantic in their quests for advancement, liberation, and emancipation. This is a story that has generally
been told within separate national and regional contexts. By reuniting
the history of people of African descent in the Atlantic diaspora with
that of people in Africa, this volume shows not just that there were
parallel events going on in different parts of the black Atlantic but that
there were important Atlantic interactions and contacts among black
communities as well. However much these Atlantic connections sprang
from individual and group aspirations, they also reflected a consciousness of the existence of a larger black world and a deliberate effort to
establish connections for common benefit. Making these connections
was important to many people during these centuries and remains of
lasting significance today.

Following a narrative introduction that brings together the histories
of the separate continents of the Atlantic are thirty-four documents
by black individuals and organizations. The documents begin with examples of black people of various origins living in Europe or traveling
there in the eighteenth and nineteenth centuries, as well as accounts
of back-to-Africa movements before 1900. The documents in the second chapter are by African Americans and Africans concerned with
regenerating Africa through religion, education, and political reform
between 1850 and 1915. The third chapter contains documents by individuals concerned with building Pan-African unity and defending black
interests during the first half of the twentieth century. The fourth
chapter contains writings about black cultural unity from the early to
the mid-twentieth century. The final chapter contains essays by Africans visiting the United States and by African Americans visiting
Africa during the twentieth century. Half of the documents are by persons born in mainland North America; African-born people and some
West Indians wrote most of the rest.

In addition to these topics, four other themes weave themselves
through the history of the black Atlantic. The first is how Western culture and white racism divided and isolated black people and how
Western culture and the fight against racial discrimination were the
mechanism for reconnecting them. The second theme is black people's
search for security and self-fulfillment, whether by emigrating or by
increasing their social and political power. The third is black people's
struggle to construct common institutions to fight racism and unwanted white dominance, exemplified by the Pan-African and anti-
colonial struggles. The final theme is black people's effort to find their

place in a common humanity. These four themes are not mutually exclusive, and many individuals and movements were involved in more than one.

Following the documents are several useful guides for understanding and evaluating the black Atlantic: a chronology of key events, questions for consideration, a selected bibliography for further reading, and an index.

## ACKNOWLEDGMENTS

This book has been a long time in the making. Its origins lie in my experiences in the 1960s of teaching in a rural Nigerian secondary school and then at Tuskegee Institute in Alabama. Both of these experiences opened worlds I had scarcely encountered in my prior education and sparked both my consciousness and my curiosity. Decades of study, reading, and teaching African and world history at Boston College deepened and broadened my knowledge and understanding. I am particularly thankful to the brave students who recently joined me in a graduate colloquium on the black Atlantic that made us all focus on this important emerging field of study.

Thanks to Elizabeth Welch and Mary Dougherty of Bedford/St. Martin's, who plied me with lavish meals until I consented to attempt this collection. Jane Knetzger and Betty Slack were ever helpful in improving the manuscript, as were the reviewers: Makungu Akinyela (Georgia State University), Kenneth Mason (Santa Monica College), G. Ugo Nwokeyji (University of California, Berkeley), Dianne White Oyler (Fayetteville State University), and Jon Sensbach (University of Florida), as well as one reviewer who wished to remain anonymous. Thanks too to Joan E. Feinberg, Katherine Meisenheimer, and Laurel Damashek of Bedford/St. Martin's for their support in the complex publishing process.

David Northrup

# Contents

## APPENDIXES

# Illustrations

THE BEDFORD SERIES IN HISTORY AND CULTURE

# Crosscurrents in the Black Atlantic, 1770–1965

## A Brief History with Documents

# PART ONE

# Introduction: Reconnecting Africa and the African Diaspora

The black Atlantic is a place and a state of mind. Geographically it includes African homelands as well as the places in Europe and the Americas to which black people have been dispersed over time. Mentally the black Atlantic refers to the rising sense of commonality among black leaders around the Atlantic based on their common origins, their shared physical and cultural traits, their common oppression, and their need to unite to gain equality. This book is about that rising consciousness and the struggle it fed.

Forced migration was the father of the black Atlantic. Torn from their homes in Africa, millions of enslaved people were transported to the far corners of the Americas (and a few to Europe). With the passage of time, the multitude of African languages and cultures they brought with them were largely overlain or displaced by the language and culture of their new communities. Even among those who had gained their freedom, harsh discrimination prevented their full assimilation into their host communities. As the great African American leader Frederick Douglass wrote, "America will not allow her children to love her" (Document 6).

Mother wit was the black Atlantic's other parent. Countless individuals lifted themselves from abject misery into at least moderate respectability by their inner determination and natural talents, aided

1

by luck and charitable patrons. Mother wit was also what led many to search out new homes where they might be free of discrimination, to forge new connections with other blacks around the Atlantic. By the second half of the eighteenth century, we can begin to document the efforts of free or otherwise empowered black people not only to better themselves but also to build connections to blacks in Europe, Africa, and the Americas so as to empower and liberate them all from discrimination. A key aspect of the black Atlantic world was the emerging awareness among black people in the Americas and Europe that they were not just Brazilians, Americans, Jamaicans, or Britons who happened to be black, but that they also shared an identity as members of an African diaspora. (A *diaspora* refers to people dispersed away from their homeland by force or other circumstances.) While those of the African diaspora were rethinking their connections to their ancestral homeland, the diverse peoples of Africa were also developing a growing sense of common identity in their efforts to overcome disabilities and were beginning to sense that they might gain from connections to their long-lost brothers and sisters in the diaspora.

This collection of readings by black people from Africa and from the diaspora details five successive stages over the first two centuries of this underappreciated saga of reconnection, liberation, and identity. (Locations mentioned are shown on the map on pages 4–5.) The selections in the first group of readings provide examples of individual efforts to escape discrimination and find fulfillment in Europe and, increasingly in the nineteenth century, in places of liberation in Africa. Readings in the second group document the efforts of black people in the diaspora during the second half of the nineteenth century to share their faith in Christianity and their love of education with their African cousins and thereby redeem Africans both spiritually and materially.

The third group of readings details the efforts, during the first part of the twentieth century, toward institutionalizing black unity through a series of "Pan-Africanist" meetings and movements that began in the Americas and spread to Europe and Africa. The fourth set of readings reveals other approaches to defining black unity and liberation during the middle decades of the twentieth century, whether as part of an international movement for human equality or as an appreciation of the interconnectedness of African and African diaspora cultures. The final set of readings consists of descriptions of six individual transatlantic voyages in the twentieth century: Three of these voyages were extended visits to the United States by young West African students who would later become important political leaders, and the other three were trips to Africa of varying length by African Americans in search of their ancestral heritage.

This survey of themes in the black Atlantic ends in the mid-twentieth century, not because it is a breaking point but because some notable shifts in the currents of the black Atlantic took place then. One was the shift of leadership in the Pan-African movement into African hands after the end of the Second World War and the subsequent liberation of most of Africa from white rule. The other was the relative success of civil rights struggles in individual countries of the Americas. More recent concerns in the black Atlantic with common identity and connections may better be understood after the passage of some additional time.

## SEEKING NEW HOMES IN EUROPE AND AFRICA, 1773–1859

Freedom, faith, and education were critical elements in the struggles of blacks in the Atlantic world. Freedom and education were in short supply for black men and women before the mid-1800s. The pioneering generation of Atlantic leaders came from the minority who had managed to acquire free status, by their own efforts and often with the help of others. Almost without exception, the pioneers of the black Atlantic were sincere Christians, not simply because it was the dominant religion of the diaspora but because, as their words and lives reveal, they found strength and fulfillment in Christianity's story of redemption and equality. The literacy and learning these pioneers acquired through education were critical in transforming their circumstances and in providing the legacy of their thoughts and achievements in the writings of this collection. Thus those we know best were decidedly an elite—educated, articulate, and gifted. A less visible underclass of free blacks also plied the Atlantic as seamen and moved across its waters, but their lives and aspirations are part of a history known indirectly, if at all.

That the greatest concentration of early records comes from black people in the English-speaking world is not surprising since Britain was the greatest slave-trading nation of the eighteenth century, and its colonies and former colonies held many slaves and some free blacks. At the end of the century, Britain also became the center of the abolitionist movement, and many Atlantic blacks owed much to sympathetic and generous white patrons there. A notable number of literary

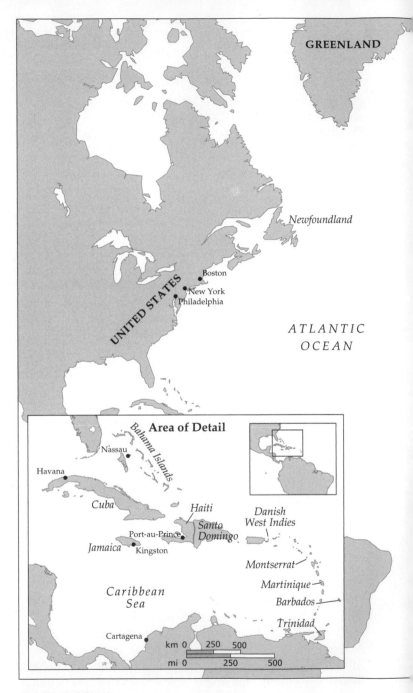

*The Black Atlantic.*

4

St. Petersburg

Belfast ENGLAND
London

Paris
FRANCE

ITALY

Madeira
Islands

Canary
Islands

SENEGAL

SIERRA
Freetown LEONE
Monrovia LIBERIA

Niger River

Yoruba

Opobo

ETHIOPIA

Congo River

CONGO
FREE
STATE

MALAWI

N
W E
S

km 0    500  1,000
mi 0      500      1,000

5

and musically accomplished blacks were drawn to the Atlantic's greatest port, London, which was home to a growing underclass.[1] Among the fortunate black elite who left us written records were Olaudah Equiano (Document 2) and Ottobah Cugoano (Document 3). The former British colonies of North America were also important. Poet Phillis Wheatley (Document 1) was a resident of Massachusetts, as was the remarkable Nancy Gardner Prince (Document 5). Both black women traveled across the Atlantic to Europe, where Prince's account reveals that there were clusters of black servants around the great courts of Europe as far east as Moscow.

Two events enhanced Britain's central place in the black Atlantic. One was the 1772 decision by Chief Justice William M. Mansfield that British law (unlike the laws in British colonies) did not recognize slavery and that the slave James Somerset could not be forced by his master to leave British soil. That ruling led many blacks to believe that residence in Britain guaranteed their freedom, although Mansfield's narrow decision did not go that far. The second event was the outcome of the American Revolutionary War. The British had promised freedom to any slave of rebellious North American colonists who would join the British side. At the war's end some of these black Loyalists accompanied British (and Hessian) troops back to Europe, while others were resettled (along with white Loyalists) in the Canadian colony of Nova Scotia.

## Sierra Leone: The Province of Freedom

The increase in the number of free blacks in Britain and British North America led to the founding of a new colony in West Africa in 1787 that became a center of black Atlantic activity. This "Province of Freedom" on the Sierra Leone coast was initially meant to be a place of refuge for London's poor black population, which had grown rapidly after the American Revolution. Like most early English colonies in the Americas, Sierra Leone was a private foundation, sponsored by investors who knew they were unlikely to reap any profit from their generous help to impoverished black people. As Equiano's and Cugoano's accounts (Documents 2 and 3) detail, the initial settlement got off to a rocky start, but it improved after the arrival in 1792 of 1,100 black "Nova Scotians" led by Thomas Peters (Document 4). Unhappy with the lands Britain had provided them in Canada, these black Loyalists from the rebel thirteen colonies of North America migrated to the new African colony.[2] In 1800 they were joined by 550 "Maroons," free African Jamaicans who had long been a thorn in the side of that British plantation colony. In 1815 Paul Cuffe, a prosperous free African American from Massachusetts, sponsored the settlement of thirty-eight African Americans in Sierra Leone, although his plans to settle two thousand more ended with his death. Along with their quest for freedom and a better life, settlers in Sierra Leone, the first outpost in Africa of blacks returning from the diaspora, brought with them a devotion to Christianity, the English language, and other aspects of Anglo-American culture.

From 1808 the colony of Sierra Leone served as the headquarters of the British Royal Navy's patrol that sought to intercept ships engaging in the now illegal slave trade across the Atlantic. Substantial numbers of Africans were rescued by British patrols from captured slave ships and then liberated and resettled in the colony. Alienated from their homes and families, many liberated Africans proved receptive to the preaching of Christian missionaries and flocked to the mission schools in the colony. Many of their teachers and co-religionists were earlier black "creoles" from England, Jamaica, and the United States. (*Creole* here refers to people born and raised outside their continent of origin and who have thus acquired a cultural identity different from that of their ancestors.) The liberated Africans and their descendants thus acquired a creole identity (later known as *Krio*) in addition to their original African identities. Some Sierra Leoneans who returned to their homelands in the middle of the nineteenth century helped spread Christianity and some Western customs to other parts of Africa. More than thirty thousand others emigrated to the British West Indies after the end of slavery in the 1830s.

## Liberia: The Second Black Colony in West Africa

In 1821 the new American Colonization Society founded the colony of Liberia, to the south of Sierra Leone, as a refuge for free blacks from the United States. The white Americans who supported this venture included some people genuinely concerned with improving the lives of free African Americans and others more concerned with reducing the free black population in the United States. After the colony became independent in 1847, the small population of African American settlers (known as Americo-Liberians and numbering about six thousand in 1850) controlled the new Republic of Liberia's fractious politics and precarious economy. Over the next several decades the troubled position of African Americans in America promoted new interest in emigration from the United States. The Fugitive Slave Law of 1850 imperiled the freedom of slaves who had managed to escape to northern states where slavery was illegal. The freeing of the huge American slave population following the Union victory in the Civil War in 1865 brought new hopes but left most former slaves in poverty and, after the collapse of Reconstruction in 1877, subject to harsh discrimination. Although the great African American abolitionist and orator Frederick Douglass vividly recounted the oppressive atmosphere of mid-nineteenth-century America (Document 6), he opposed emigration to Africa on the grounds that two and a half centuries in North America had turned Africans into Americans.

For that and other reasons the number of new settlers in Liberia remained small. Those who went there were often disappointed by the colony's lack of opportunities and faced health challenges from living in a tropical environment. Except for missionary efforts, relations between Americo-Liberians and their African neighbors did not yield positive results, which was hardly surprising since most settlers regarded the indigenous people as "wild and untutored savages" (Document 7).

In some cases, however, emigration to Liberia had satisfying outcomes for both settler and native African. A notable example is that of the African Jaja (Njojo) (1821–1891), who was enslaved as a youth in southern Nigeria and sold from his Igbo homeland to Africans in the chief Niger Delta port of Bonny. A generation earlier he would have been sold into the Atlantic, but with the transatlantic slave trade at an end Bonny had repositioned itself as West Africa's chief port for palm oil. Jaja became the slave of one of the "canoe houses" (African companies) that bought palm oil from the inland waterside markets and sold it in bulk to the British traders who flocked to Bonny. His talent and intelligence enabled him to advance rapidly to a middle management position and then to the head of the canoe house. As head of the house that owned him, Jaja was no longer a slave in fact but was still looked down on by the free citizens of Bonny. After a dispute in 1869 Jaja moved his operations to the port of Opobo.

Emma White (ca. 1845–ca. 1890) was also a slave in her early life in Louisville, Kentucky, where she was born. She had converted to Methodism in her youth and had somehow managed to get a solid education. After the Civil War she joined the trickle of emancipated African Americans seeking to build new lives in Liberia. Taking advantage of the regular shipping lines that growing trade had brought to West Africa, White made a precarious living trading from one port to another. In 1875 she reached Opobo, where she remained for most of the next dozen years in Jaja's service.

Jaja was eager that his children would have advantages denied to him, especially the education needed to succeed in West Africa's rapidly changing world. He sent one son to be educated in Glasgow, a daughter to Liverpool, and several others to missionary schools in the British colonies of Lagos and Sierra Leone. In 1873 he had opened a school in Opobo headed by a Sierra Leonean man named Gooding. Impressed with Emma White's education and knowledge of the world, Jaja hired her as his secretary (replacing another Sierra Leonean) and as the new head of his school. Under her direction the school won high praise from European visitors for its quality.

Emma White also became Jaja's trusted adviser on the ways of the British people who were his customers and his models for modernizing Opobo. Her own thoughts are largely unknown, but she was clearly devoted to Jaja and tried without success to convince him of the value of Christianity. Returning to Opobo in 1881 after a two-year absence, she regained Jaja's favor and patronage. In this period she became known as Emma Jaja Johnson, in tribute to her patron and in recognition of her marriage to an Opobo man named Johnson.

Black people in the diaspora had a variety of views about returning to Africa. Cugoano supported the idea of the Sierra Leonean settlement but was sympathetic to the reluctance of many blacks in Britain to return to Africa so long as the Atlantic slave trade was still in existence. Equiano was another strong supporter of the Sierra Leone project, but, though they both identified themselves as Africans, Cugoano and Equiano remained in Britain. Starting in the 1840s, free blacks in Brazil began returning to the Yoruba and Hausa homelands (now in Nigeria) from which they had been sold and whose language and culture they remembered. Despite years of absence, they reassimilated to their African homeland in most ways.

# MISSIONS TO REDEEM AFRICA, 1853–1891

Alienated from their ancestral homeland by much longer spans of time, other blacks from the diaspora discovered that cultural obstacles blocked their reintegration in Africa. They did not speak any African language and were generally unaware of what particular part of Africa their ancestors had come from. Moreover, their images of African culture were often highly negative. Under the influence of Christianity many in the diaspora had rationalized the terrible ordeal of enslavement and transport to the Americas as part of a divine plan to bring them to Christianity. The most highly motivated now saw it as their duty to bring the Gospel to Africa. The idea of redeeming Africa, voiced a century earlier by Cugoano and Equiano, was central to the thinking of Edward Wilmot Blyden, one of the strongest supporters of Liberian immigration (Document 10). A free black from the Danish West Indies, Blyden had emigrated to Liberia after being refused admission to a theological college in New Jersey on account of his race.

Debates about the wisdom of emigrating often incorporated ideas of redeeming Africa. Richard Allen, the first bishop of the African Methodist Episcopal (AME) Church, an African American denomination, was a strong opponent of the Liberian venture but supported emigration to Haiti, as did President Abraham Lincoln. With characteristic pragmatism, the eminent African American educator Booker T. Washington dismissed the emigrationist position as no solution to African Americans' problems, pointing out that on the same day that six hundred blacks sailed from Savannah, Georgia, for Liberia, an equal number of African American children were born in the black belt of the South.[3]

Other African American leaders who regarded America as their cultural home embraced emigration as a way to escape America's intolerable racism. One of the leading spokesmen for emigration was the AME bishop Henry McNeal Turner, who agreed with the sentiments of both Douglass and Washington but concluded that disenfranchisement and discrimination had robbed African Americans of their birthright. He wrote in 1883: "We were born here, raised here, fought, bled and died here, and have a thousand times more right here than hundreds of thousands of those who help to snub, proscribe and persecute us, and this is one of the reasons I almost despise the land of my birth."[4] Turner never envisioned a total exodus of African Americans to Africa; rather he favored the gradual assemblage of a critical mass in Africa who would build a "civilized, Christian" nation there (Document 11). Another distinguished African American, Dr. Martin J. Delany, initially opposed all emigration, arguing, as did Douglass, that the Americas were African Americans' true home, but the onerousness of the Fugitive Slave Law of 1850 drove him to reverse his position. Delany's solution was to search out places in Africa that had escaped colonization by Europeans or Africans and remained under traditional African leaders (Document 8). Another medical doctor, James Africanus Horton, a Sierra Leonean descended from liberated Africans, also believed that existing African states were capable of modernizing themselves, and, like Jaja, he saw no need for outsiders to play a leading role in that process.[5]

As Bishop Turner clearly illustrated, the image of Africa as a place of refuge from racial discrimination was entwined with the belief that African Americans' duty was to "redeem" Africans by converting them to Christianity, educating them, and introducing them to the moral and social values then prevalent in the Western world. Though white missionaries also undertook such work in Africa, many black missions were an outgrowth of the roles that black churches in the post-emancipation American South and the West Indies were playing in lifting people out of poverty and ignorance. Thus it was natural for some African American leaders to look across the Atlantic to Africa as a place to repeat this effort at uplifting black folk. Both black and white missionaries assumed that their sustained efforts were needed to correct the enduring negative effects of the Atlantic slave trade. The AME Church was in the forefront of these movements, although African American missionaries also served many other black-led and white-led enterprises. By 1900 some eighty-six African American missionaries had served or were serving in African missions, the vast majority in Liberia and Sierra Leone.[6] In 1893 the American Missionary Association sponsored a "World Congress on Africa," at which Bishop Turner pushed for further African American involvement in Africa.

Christian missions in Africa were not entirely in the hands of persons born outside the continent. Before 1850 a number of Africans from Brazil and Cuba, now free from slavery, had returned to their southern Nigerian homes, bringing Roman Catholic practices with them. Other Christian African converts returned from Sierra Leone, and missionaries soon followed them. A remarkable liberated African, Samuel Ajayi Crowther, a passionate advocate for education and a devout Christian, was ordained as an Anglican bishop in 1864 and placed in charge of the evangelization of the peoples of the lower Niger River. As his charge to his African and European clergy in 1869 illustrates (Document 12), he strongly endorsed their joint enterprise in the mission work but also sought respect for some African customs.

Another place where Africans were deeply involved in the redemption of Africa before 1900 was the Cape Colony in southern Africa. As a consequence of both peaceful and turbulent interactions with an expanding European settler frontier in the 1800s, many black South Africans became Christians, acquired Western educations, and began to seek contacts with other black Christians. Racial discrimination in the colony led to the division of many churches along color lines and encouraged many black leaders there to join with other black people in the fight for equality. In 1896 one group of black churches in the Cape Colony sent a delegation to the United States that agreed to unite with the AME Church. They also issued a call for African American missionaries and teachers to come to southern Africa. Bishop Turner visited in 1898 and promoted the union. Despite resistance from white political authorities in the self-governing Cape Colony and some African defection from the new unified church, African Americans were instrumental in the opening of new black churches and schools there.

## THE QUEST FOR UNITY, LIBERATION, AND ADVANCEMENT, 1897–1958

As a consequence of these missionary connections, some African students went to the United States for advanced education. One study has uncovered information on sixty-eight students from Africa who studied in the United States by 1900. They came from seven different territories, with Liberia supplying nearly half and South Africa and Sierra Leone accounting for most of the rest. Lincoln University in Pennsylvania accepted the first college students (nine from Liberia in 1873, all of whom were indigenous Africans) and subsequently admitted many more. Other Africans were welcomed by other traditionally black schools, including Fisk University, Wilberforce University, Livingstone College, and Morris Brown College. Some of these pioneering students went on to distinguished careers: John L. Dube, who had studied at Oberlin College in Ohio, and Pixley ka Isaka Seme, who had been a student at the Mount Hermon School in Massachusetts, were two of the founders of the South African Native National Congress (later the African National Congress). Seme in 1901 had founded a school in Natal modeled on Booker T. Washington's Tuskegee Institute and had called upon all blacks in southern Africa to unite in opposing white racism (Document 17).[7]

Attitudes of blacks in the diaspora toward Africa were shifting in the late nineteenth century. Older leaders, such as the pioneering

African American missionary Alexander Crummell (Document 9), saw Africa as a pagan and barbarous land to be rescued, if necessary, by European colonial rule. An interesting transitional figure was George Washington Williams, a distinguished African American who moved from being an enthusiastic supporter of the Congo Free State's "civilizing mission" in central Africa to being a sharp critic of its defects (Document 13).

Although a sense of Christian mission by no means disappeared, from the late nineteenth century there was growing stress on the notion of Africa as a homeland and a growing belief that Africans possessed valid cultural traditions and were fully equal human beings. Despite more positive images of Africa, a large cultural gulf between the New World "Negroes" and Africans remained. While Blyden referred to blacks like himself as being "in exile," he also stressed the "incalculable advantage" those in the diaspora had gained from contact with "the dominant race"—Christianity, education, and the English language being among those advantages. The shifting priorities are more clearly apparent in the ideas of the Jamaican black activist Marcus Garvey and his briefly powerful Universal Negro Improvement Association (UNIA) (Documents 18 and 19). Garvey and the UNIA were solidly in favor of African self-determination, of "Africa for the Africans" (which included all people of full African ancestry wherever they might live), although he also stressed the value of Christian worship and formal education in raising "the fallen of the race." The support for African liberation grew stronger among diaspora blacks throughout the twentieth century.

To a great extent this shift in priorities found parallel among Atlantic Africans, among whom a rising eagerness for advanced formal education, Christianity, and fluency in European languages was tied to a rising eagerness to liberate themselves from colonial rule. After 1900 growing numbers of African students made their way to the United States to study at traditional black colleges, such as Booker T. Washington's Tuskegee Institute in Alabama (Document 15), and to the few white institutions that would admit and subsidize black students. Given the influence of Dr. Washington's strategies in the American South and in Africa, it is instructive to consider the strong criticism of his nonconfrontational approach by the other leading African American intellectual of his day, W. E. B. Du Bois (Document 16).

Combined with the personal fulfillment that such educational advancement brought was a strengthening commitment to using that education for group liberation from white rule. This sentiment was strongest in South Africa at the beginning of the century (Document 17) and grew more widespread after 1945. There and elsewhere the passion for unity and freedom had a potential for violence, as can be seen in the career of the American-trained Baptist minister John Chilembwe of Nyasaland, whose passion for an African Christian Union in 1897 (Document 14) led him to armed rebellion in 1915.

## Early Pan-Africanism

Differences and misunderstandings were impediments to black unity, but in the first half of the twentieth century black leaders in the Atlantic showed remarkable determination to build institutions that would enable them to fight the racial discrimination that held them all back. Although it has been suggested that the missionary-sponsored World Congress on Africa of 1893 in Chicago should be counted as the start of the Pan-Africanist movement,[8] most historians regard the more secular Pan-African meeting in London in 1900 as the true beginning of the movement for black unity. At that assembly, called by British West Indians and others under the leadership of Henry Sylvester Williams, an Afro-Trinidadian lawyer, delegates formed a permanent Pan-African Association to promote the rights and progress of African people throughout the world.

Although important symbolically, the small Pan-African Association had less impact than the Universal Negro Improvement Association founded by Marcus Garvey in his native Jamaica in 1914.[9] The UNIA's manifesto stated its sweeping goals:

> To establish a Universal Confraternity among the race; to promote the spirit of race pride and love; to reclaim the fallen of the race; to administer to and assist the needy; to assist in civilizing the backward tribes of Africa; . . . to promote a conscientious Christian worship among the native tribes of Africa; to establish Universities, Colleges and Secondary Schools for the further education and culture of the boys and girls of the race; to conduct world-wide commercial and industrial intercourse.[10]

When Garvey moved to New York in 1916, he found an audience readily receptive to his ideas of black greatness and the need to build institutions to raise the profile and power of black people. Membership in the UNIA soared. Garvey is a hard figure to summarize, in part because he incorporated both old and new approaches to Africa. His program of Christianity, education, and uplift reflected the work of

Booker T. Washington, the reading of whose autobiography, *Up from Slavery*, Garvey said had "doomed" him to his course of action.

Yet as an institution builder Garvey broke new ground. Garvey's frequent references to "Africa for the Africans" (a slogan also used by Chilembwe) illustrated the universalism of his thinking. The UNIA soon had more than thirty branches and tens of thousands of members. Garvey revived plans for back-to-Africa settlements in Liberia, the Congo, and Ethiopia. In 1919 he founded the Black Star Line (whose name echoes that of the leading transatlantic British passenger company, the White Star Line) in furtherance of his worldwide shipping ambitions. The UNIA newspaper *The Negro World*, founded a year earlier, had a circulation in the tens of thousands; passed from hand to hand and read aloud, it reached a much larger audience. Editions in Spanish and French targeted a larger Atlantic audience. A contemporary critic described *The Negro World* as "the best edited colored weekly in New York," and a modern historian deemed it "one of the most remarkable journalistic ventures ever attempted by a Negro in the United States."[11] The efforts by governments in Central America and Africa to ban it testify to the paper's power. Widespread rumors in South Africa and Southern Rhodesia of the pending arrival of a black fleet (or an air force in another version) to liberate the masses from white rule led governments to prohibit entry not only of Garvey himself and copies of *The Negro World* but also of nearly all African Americans, who were thought to be agents of radicalism. Such prohibition did not stem Garvey's popularity. The great South African labor organizer Clements Kadalie, who declared his goal "to be the African Marcus Garvey," built a powerful trade union movement in the industrial cities of South Africa in the 1920s that was as large (and as short-lived) as Garvey's movement.[12]

The UNIA's rapid growth and large (often imprudent) financial investments alarmed the American government as well as many moderate African American leaders. Du Bois was a great supporter of the Pan-African movement, but he found Garvey "bombastic and impractical." After Garvey was convicted of mail fraud in 1925 and deported to Jamaica two years later, his movement declined, but its memory lived on. In the meantime Garvey had derailed Du Bois's Pan-African Congress movement. The decline was already evident by the time of the third Congress in London in 1923, and the fourth in 1927 in New York has been described as "an empty gesture to keep the idea alive."[13] From that point leadership in the black Atlantic world began to slip out of North American hands.

Before moving on to consider that later Pan-Africanism, we should reflect on the very different agendas and impacts of the three most prominent African diaspora leaders of the first half of the twentieth century: Booker T. Washington, the pragmatic educator; W. E. B. Du Bois, the urbane intellectual; and Marcus Garvey, the fiery, populist organizer. Of the three, Washington was the least preoccupied with Africa—his preoccupation was the uplifting of African Americans, especially in the rural South, but he arguably had the greatest impact on Africans who wished to imitate Tuskegee's success (Document 15). Du Bois was much more concerned with Africans, and his pioneering work, *The World and Africa: An Inquiry into the Part Which Africa Has Played in World History* (1947), was very instrumental in bringing a positive image of African history and culture to African American readers. Du Bois chose to die in Africa and was buried there. Yet this symbolic expression of his Pan-African beliefs had no more impact on Africans than did the many other actions of his enormously productive life. That cannot be said about Garvey. His efforts to found colonies of African Americans in Liberia and Ethiopia and his Black Star shipping line were real, if transitory, connections to Africa. Moreover, the symbolism of what Garvey was trying to do had enormous impact on African leaders and masses.

**Later Pan-Africanism**

After Garvey's deportation from the United States, the Pan-Africanist gloss on African Americans' struggle for equality was less in evidence. Two notable exceptions were the concern for the fate of Ethiopia in the 1930s (see below) and the activities of the Council on African Affairs (CAA), established in 1937 to influence American policies toward Africa. The CAA's two African American leaders were Paul Robeson, a multitalented entertainer and activist, and Max Yergen, a committed member of the YMCA with much African experience. Like black liberation leaders in South Africa, Europe, and the West Indies (see Document 20), the CAA regarded anti-imperialist Communists as their allies. To punish Robeson for his "leftist internationalism," the U.S. government deprived him of his American passport.

The CAA organized a Conference on Africa in New York City in 1944 that raised a range of issues about Africa's future. However, it was not that meeting but the Pan-African conference in Manchester, England, in 1945 that is remembered as a milestone in the black rights struggle. The meeting was organized by the Pan-African Federation, a new coalition of black organizations in Great Britain and Africa. Robeson and Yergen were invited to Manchester, but they did not attend, apparently because the American Communist party opposed the meeting. W. E. B. Du Bois went as an observer, but, in contrast to earlier Pan-African meetings that had been led by West Indians and Americans, the Manchester conference was dominated by a younger generation of Western-educated Africans, who would soon be leading their countries to independence. At a time when anticolonialism was still weak in the United States, it was the major theme of the Manchester meeting. One of the participating organizations was the International African Service Bureau (IASB), which had been organized in Britain in 1937 in the wake of the League of Nations' failure to defend Ethiopia. The IASB's strong West Indian and African leadership included the Trinidadian George Padmore, the Nigerian Nnamdi Azikiwe (Document 30), and the Kenyan Jomo Kenyatta. Along with other publications, it sponsored a journal, edited by another talented Trinidadian, C. L. R. James (Document 20). Not surprisingly, this Pan-African conference focused much of its attention on the problems of African colonies, particularly those run by Britain. Resolutions called unambiguously for African independence and self-rule (Document 21).

While the Manchester meeting was a watershed for Pan-Africanism, the movement for black liberation still had a long way to go. Yet in the next fifteen years events moved faster than anyone could have predicted. Six years after the Manchester conference that he co-chaired with George Padmore, Kwame Nkrumah was elected head of government in the Gold Coast Colony. After returning to Nigeria, Nnamdi Azikiwe resumed his career in politics and journalism and became the first prime minister of Nigeria in 1960. After spending most of the 1950s in detention in Kenya for his alleged (and unproven) involvement in the "Mau Mau" uprising, Jomo Kenyatta emerged to win the first election as Kenya's president in 1963. By then Pan-Africanism had become a decidedly African movement, centered on the needs of that continent's emerging nations, but it is notable that all three of these African leaders had been strongly influenced by experiences elsewhere in the Atlantic. As students in the United States, Nkrumah and Azikiwe had been involved in African American issues and institutions. Kenyatta had spent many years in Britain and, like the others, had impressive achievements in higher education. The dissertation he wrote for his doctorate in anthropology from the University of London was published as *Facing Mount Kenya: The Tribal Life of the Gikuyu.*

## BLACK CULTURAL UNITY AND GLOBAL AGENDAS, 1904–1966

Debates about black cultural unity echoed around the Atlantic in the middle years of the twentieth century. If political leadership was in the hands of an elite, these cultural debates were the product of an even smaller group of intellectuals, but their impact far exceeded their numbers.

To a large extent black intellectuals were divided along linguistic lines. In the large camp of English-speaking blacks, the idea of unity was based on race. Blyden, Garvey, and Du Bois were all "race men," obsessed with the idea of an underlying black unity based on black skin and African blood. Some proponents, such as Blyden, were also obsessed with ideas of racial purity and were highly suspicious of individuals who had any non-African ancestors. In retrospect, these ideas seem to be strongly influenced by the prevailing racial ideas among white people, with African purity substituted for black inferiority. This aspect troubled some. In Document 26, Du Bois reflects on his changing ideas about race and the way racial discrimination fostered a bond among black people.

Another approach to black unity stressed culture. It argued that, despite the differences the diaspora had created, black people shared a common cultural heritage. Music was one of the first areas of culture in which this was explored, as in the early work of Samuel Coleridge-Taylor (Document 24). Later studies of African aesthetics and patterns of thinking also focused attention on cultural commonality, for example, the essay on African music by the celebrated black singer and actor Paul Robeson (Document 25). The African American literary movement of the 1920s known as the "Harlem Renaissance" or the "New Negro Movement" had a similar concern with black culture as a defining force. This cultural approach was also pervasive among blacks growing up in French colonies, hardly surprising since the French emphasize culture in defining their nation and civilization.

### Négritude

The movement in the black Francophone world was more decidedly literary and philosophical than its counterpart in the Anglophone world. It came to center on the new word *négritude*, which the French West Indian poet Aimé Césaire had employed in his 1939 poem "Cahier d'un retour au pays natal" ("Notebook of a Return to the

Native Land"), about his contemplated return to his native island of Martinique in the French West Indies after a long residence in Paris. As the poet explained in an interview (Document 27), in the colonies the French word *nègre* was nearer in meaning to "nigger" than to the later usage as equivalent to "Negro" or "black" that the *négritude* movement espoused. In choosing to use *négritude* as a term of black pride and identity, Césaire meant to challenge white racism and build black pride.

The great Senegalese poet and politician Léopold Senghor took up and elaborated upon the meaning of *négritude*, and he, along with others, made it the center of a black pride movement. From one perspective, Senghor might be seen as an odd champion of distinctively African cultural traits, for he was both legally and in practice a person profoundly assimilated into French culture. He wrote affectionately of *la Francophonie* (the French-speaking community) and *la Francité* (the distinctively logical French way of thinking). Though an African, he spoke and wrote exclusively in French and, before becoming president of Senegal, held a seat in the French National Assembly reserved for a delegate from the assimilated minority of Senegalese Africans. Yet, from another point of view, Senghor greatly resembled his Anglophone counterparts in the United States who rhapsodized about Africa precisely because it was so alien to their own experience. Interestingly, many black intellectuals in Africa were critical of the disconnect between the extremely French demeanor of these intellectuals and their advocacy of *négritude*. "I don't think a tiger has to go around proclaiming his tigritude," mocked the Nigerian writer Wole Soyinka, who in 1986 was awarded the Nobel Prize in literature.[14]

In his 1966 essay (Document 28), Senghor replied to some of this criticism, arguing that the roots of *négritude* lay in the African American cultural movement, a point that Césaire also acknowledged. As his essay makes clear, Senghor was well read in the intellectual and literary works of blacks in the Americas. Césaire had written a dissertation on the Harlem Renaissance. Indeed, it might be said that the similarities between Francophone and Anglophone cultural movements were more profound than either Senghor or Césaire realized— as were the differences. The fusion of race identity and cultural identity was common to the thought of many less sophisticated and less literary English-speaking blacks. Both Blyden and Garvey were profoundly "race men" in their thinking, but the ideas and institutions of these West Indians had scarcely penetrated the French Caribbean or the intellectual debates of West Africans in Paris. *Négritude* was a distinctly elite intellectual movement whose Western roots found little resonance among the African masses.

A third approach to black integration, which transcended both race and culture, lay in the growing internationalism of the twentieth century. Despite his commitment to *négritude* and to a distinctively African personality, Senghor saw pride in one's blackness as a step toward the larger goal of gaining acceptance for blacks as equal human beings. Du Bois made a similar point in his 1940 essay (Document 26). In contrast to narrower thinking, those who embraced internationalism or humanism sought to gain equal membership for black people in a world in which color and cultural differences were an irrational division. This frame of mind is evident in the selections from Haile Selassie (Document 22) and Ralph J. Bunche (Document 23), both of whom struggled to fight racism in a global arena.

## Crises in Liberia and Ethiopia

The transatlantic connections between Africa and the black diaspora were troubled during the first half of the twentieth century by particular events. Given the serious local problems of discrimination and poverty all black communities faced, Pan-African dreams were not at the top of most black people's agendas, but on occasion the news from Africa was dramatic enough to excite interest in the diaspora. The crises in Liberia in the 1920s and Ethiopia in the 1930s were such events, but unfortunately neither crisis led to a resolution clear and positive enough to sustain transatlantic interest.

Liberia had been controversial among African Americans from the beginning. A century after its founding the country continued to present conflicting images. On the one hand, it was a beacon of black independence and self-rule; on the other, it was a colony where Westernized black people lorded it over an African majority and failed to fulfill their pledges to improve the Africans' welfare. Liberia came under a great deal of criticism in the 1920s as details of labor contracts signed by Africans under a government arrangement with Firestone Rubber Company revealed a situation tantamount to unfree labor. Some prominent African American leaders such as Du Bois rushed to Liberia's defense, but the scandal led to a League of Nations condemnation that drove the Liberian president out of office and dimmed Liberia's image as a symbol of freedom and progress.

Ethiopia presented a different but equally contradictory set of circumstances. As the oldest continuous government in Africa, it represented black achievement and ancient glories, but it was also a desperately poor feudal monarchy with a troubled history of serfdom and slave trading that continued well into the twentieth century. Emperor Haile Selassie, who ascended the throne in 1930, positioned himself as a reformer successfully enough to gain Ethiopia's admission to the League of Nations, but he also had to deal with entrenched and resistant noble and ecclesiastical interests. The Italian government of Benito Mussolini exploited this situation, successfully laying claim to the coastal province of Eritrea and negotiating a peace treaty with Ethiopia in 1928, under whose cover plans were laid for Italy to claim the entire kingdom in the name of civilization and reform. When in 1935–1936 the Italian air force used explosives and poison gas to devastate the kingdom, Selassie made a desperate appeal to the Council of the League of Nations to save his people and the international structure that the League represented (Document 22). Unlike Cetshwayo, the exiled king of the Zulu who in 1882 had pointedly asked the British, "Do you kill me thus because I am black?" Selassie never mentioned color as an issue, but the Italian-Ethiopian crisis was seen in clearly racial terms by African Americans who held vigils and prayer meetings and raised money for Ethiopian relief. The large black population of New York City was especially energized, and rallies in Harlem and Madison Square Garden in August and September 1936 attracted tens of thousands. When the League refused to act, it not only signed its own death warrant but also further dampened the interest in African affairs among diaspora blacks.

## TRANSATLANTIC VOYAGERS, 1914–1963

Emerging similarities in the aspirations of Africans and their diaspora cousins enhanced their abilities to communicate, but among the masses on both sides of the ocean ignorance and cultural misunderstanding was still widespread. James Aggrey, a student from the Gold Coast Colony (later Ghana), found "prejudice and superstition" about Africa rife among his fellow graduate students (all white) at Columbia University in 1914 (Document 29). In passages not included in Document 31, Constance Cummings-John of Sierra Leone told of Cornell University students in 1936 who asked her, "Please show us your tail; . . . tell us if you are afraid of the lions and leopards and tigers at home in your village." She also recounted how she castigated a black missionary in a black church for describing her country as inhabited by benighted savages and cannibals.[15] In parts of southern Africa in the early 1900s, a more positive image of African Americans as military liberators spread widely due to a distorted understanding of the struggles then under way in the United States. Understanding on both sides improved over time, but differences too strong to be overcome by goodwill alone still remained at the end of the twentieth century.

Africans who traveled to Europe or the Americas in the twentieth century often found much that was surprising and much that pleased or displeased them. But they came with advantages that diaspora blacks who ventured to Africa nearly always lacked. Before crossing the physical barrier of the Atlantic, Africans had already partly traversed its cultural barrier by acquiring Western education, religion, and languages. Constance Cummings-John's family spoke English at home, and she bristled when it was suggested that she must have another primary language. Most black people born and raised in the diaspora had to confront a much wider cultural divide when they crossed the Atlantic to Africa. With rare exceptions, they were ignorant of African languages, customs, and social structures. An open mind and a tolerant outlook helped to bridge the cultural gap, but they soon discovered that wanting to be one with Africa was not enough to make that dream a reality.

Africans' comfort in the Americas may also have been aided by the fact that most came for education, not just to advance themselves but to advance the liberation of their compatriots. James Aggrey's description of his graduate classes at Columbia University in 1914 (Document 29) clearly revealed his pride in his ability to compete successfully with white students as well as his diligence and devotion to learning. Besides being a learner, Aggrey was a teacher and a preacher in New York, who successfully challenged the racial prejudices of his classmates. Aggrey helped inspire the young Nnamdi Azikiwe (future president of Nigeria) to further his education in America. There "Zik" displayed similar pride in his studies at traditionally black schools and was also a pioneering teacher of African history at Lincoln University (Document 30). A natural Pan-Africanist, Zik made alliances with black American and West Indian students but chose to leave the comforts of an American academic life to return to Nigeria and join the struggle for independence.

Like Kwame Nkrumah, who became very involved in organizing the 1945 Pan-African Congress in Manchester after his studies in the United States (Document 21), Constance Cummings-John also worked for organizations promoting Pan-African connections, once her studies were completed (Document 31). In these activities both were following in the footsteps of Dr. Aggrey.

Africans coming to the United States faced many hardships and had a lot to learn about American life and unhealthy race relations, but, as Eslanda Goode Robeson makes clear (Document 32), African Americans going to Africa for the first time often had an even more difficult time. Even for someone well educated and well informed, news of Africa in America was thin, and prejudicial ideas about Africa were dense. Robeson also needed to confront the reality that her education and upbringing had made her culturally a Westerner, even though her biological heritage and intellectual proclivities made her want to be an African. The pictures of her and young Pauli in their pith helmets show how hard it was to "go African," but her text and many photos of Africans high and low are evidence of a sincere effort to bridge the cultural divide.

Despite the obstacles, the Robesons seem to have had a good time in Africa in the 1930s; it is hard to reach the same conclusion when reading Era Bell Thompson's account (Document 33) of her African tour two decades later. A reporter for the pioneering black magazine *Ebony*, Thompson was repeatedly declared an undesirable immigrant by nervous colonial officials, who sent her out of the territory on the next plane. Her desire to stay in the best hotels meant that she often ran up against the colonial color bar. Yet, her sense of irony and her journalist's regard for the facts make her account refreshing: Ethiopia, she noted, was "Africa's oldest independent and most primitive country." One is not surprised, however, when she realistically concluded, "Africa, the land of my fathers, is not my home."[16]

Maya Angelou had the advantages of visiting an African country (Ghana) under African rule and spending a long time in one place rather than doing the grand tour. She also found that memories of her rural relatives helped her bridge the cultural gap when meeting rural Africans. While Angelou adored Ghana and Ghanaians, she, like Thompson, had no illusions that at some profound level in Africa she was an expatriate (Document 34).

## CONCLUDING OBSERVATIONS

What sense can one make of these Atlantic movements and connections? What was their historic importance for black people? Let us consider three issues.

## 1. How Successful Were the Movements for Creating Black Atlantic Unity?

Although the many individuals documented in this book achieved much with their lives and contributed much to their contemporaries, transatlantic connections remained weak, and uniting the people of Africa and the diaspora was an illusory goal. Only a tiny proportion of New World blacks returned to Africa, and hardly any of those who did so successfully reintegrated themselves into African societies and cultures. In the nineteenth century most of them were loath to accept Africans as equals unless they abandoned their African customs and beliefs. Liberia did become a black-ruled state at a time when those were an endangered species, but as in its sister republic, Haiti, poverty and corruption made it a feeble beacon of hope. The Pan-Africanist movement fought a long struggle to bring about black unity, but it succeeded best when it dropped the pretense of being an Atlantic (or larger) association and became an exclusively African movement.

From an African perspective, developments were more productive. Large numbers of Atlantic Africans embraced Christianity and the formal education brought to them by missionaries black and white. The languages and learning from abroad were instrumental in helping Africans fulfill the Pan-African dream of ending colonial rule and in forging international ties among independent African nations. The founding of the Organization of African Unity in 1963 and its successor, the African Union, were notable Pan-African achievements, even though these African successes eclipsed the New World leadership of the movement and underscored the split between Africans and people of African descent in the diaspora.

From a different perspective, the greatest achievements of the black Atlantic have come in national contexts both in Africa and in the diaspora. We should keep in mind that the currents of the black Atlantic were part of much larger struggles under way in international systems, social movements, and prevailing ideologies. This realization leads to a second question about the scope of black Atlantic interactions.

## 2. How Representative of the Black Atlantic World Were These Leaders?

The individuals represented in this book of readings were undoubtedly exceptional. Unusually bright, articulate, energetic, and committed, they stood head and shoulders above their contemporaries and were usually ahead of their times, which is why so many of their writings still resonate with readers today. At a time when white racism was the norm and black ability was deemed low, many of them awed even white listeners, who, if they were not willing to abandon their prejudices, were at least willing to make an exception for the black individual in question. How large a following did these black leaders attract? Answering a question about the masses is never easy, which is why so much of history is about exceptional individuals. None commanded a majority; few had large followings. Marcus Garvey's UNIA was a key exception: It attracted members and generated excitement all around the Atlantic. Unfortunately its life as an organization was short.

Would any of these people have disagreed with this assessment? Many openly appealed to an elite, such as Du Bois's notion that black leadership represented a "talented tenth" (a percent that was probably inflated), and Booker T. Washington had a similar idea of creating a black elite, if at a less intellectual level. Missionaries were elitists almost by definition, believing that others were gravely mistaken while they themselves had a firm grasp of the truth. Black intellectuals and political leaders had a somewhat similar view. The historical point, of course, is that the vision and energy of these exceptional individuals were supposed to mobilize, if not the masses, then at least the more thoughtful individuals. The answer is in our final question.

### 3. What Is the Legacy of These Atlantic Crossings?

The gap between those born in Africa and those born in the diaspora has always been significant. Whether it narrowed or widened after 1965 is a debatable question. In some significant ways the cultural divide between Africans and their kin in the diaspora has narrowed as Africans have achieved Western educations, mastered European languages, and become members of professions, including university posts as professors of Black Studies. Those of African descent in the diaspora have become correspondingly more likely to sport items of African dress, to wear "Afro" hair styles, to collect African art, to incorporate African elements in festivals such as Kwanzaa, or even to give themselves and their children African names.

Moreover, African American leaders have affected political developments in Africa. After the main wave of African independence crested in the mid-1960s, attention focused on the white settler colonies of southern Africa. The simultaneous rise of black voters and elected black representation in the United States made it politically impossible by the 1980s for members of Congress to accept President Reagan's efforts to water down sanctions against South Africa. The override of Reagan's veto of the congressional sanctions law, the independence of Namibia from South African rule in 1990, and the freeing of Nelson Mandela from prison in 1990 and his election in 1994 as president of South Africa represented a triumph for black Atlantic activism (and of much activism by members of the white Atlantic, too). But the momentum could not be sustained.

Black pride and romantic ideas about Africa are alive and well in the diaspora, but hard information may be in short supply. A modern study by the African American historian Ibrahim Sundiata cites the chilling statistic that in 1957, when African nationalist movements were gaining solid strength, 70 percent of African Americans could not name a single African territory and only 1 percent could list five or more African territories. He goes on to cite a 1990 poll of African American leaders, 47 percent of whom were of the opinion that "very few black Americans feel a close connection to Africa," although 90 percent of this elite group felt that they ought to influence U.S. foreign policy on behalf of Africa.[17] In his sensitive book *Kinship: A Family Journey in Africa and America*, the late Philippe Wamba—African American on his mother's side, African on his father's—describes his frustrating experiences at Harvard University in the late 1980s. The elite African American students he met there, he reported, were comfortable with superficial symbols of Africa, but profoundly uninterested in African political affairs and inclined to find the sophisticated and intellectual Wamba "too white" to fit their image of what an African was supposed to be.[18] Things may have gotten worse. In the wake of Mandela's election as South African president, the two most important American news publications devoted to African affairs, *Africa Report* and *Africa News*, both ceased publication for lack of interest.

The large migration of black people to the United States in recent years may signal the beginning of a remarkable new chapter in transatlantic black connections. Between 1960 and 2004 more than 800,000 sub-Saharan Africans arrived in the United States legally. This is more than double the number brought from Africa to the same territory during the centuries of the Atlantic slave trade. In the same period nearly 1.5 million people of African descent moved from the West Indies to the United States. By 2000 more than a quarter of black residents of Miami, Baltimore, Boston, and New York were foreign-born.[19] How these new Atlantic crossings will shape Pan-African connections and identities is an open question.

# NOTES

[1] See Gretchen Gerzina, *Black London: Life before Emancipation* (New Brunswick, N.J.: Rutgers University Press, 1995).

[2] Ellen Gibson Wilson, *The Loyal Blacks* (New York: G. P. Putnam's Sons, 1976).

[3] "An Address before the National Educational Association," Charleston, S.C., July 11, 1900, in *The Booker T. Washington Papers*, ed. Louis R. Harlan and Raymond W. Smock (Urbana: University of Illinois Press, 1976), 5:575.

[4] Turner to *Christian Recorder*, 22 Feb. 1883, quoted in Edwin S. Redkey, *Black Exodus: Black Nationalist and Back-to-Africa Movements, 1890–1910* (New Haven, Conn.: Yale University Press, 1969), 32.

[5] James Africanus Beale Horton, *West African Countries and Peoples, British and Native. With the Requirements Necessary for Establishing That Self-Government Recommended by the Committee of the House of Commons, 1865; and a Vindication of the African Race* (London: Johnson, 1868).

[6] Walter L. Williams, *Black Americans and the Evangelization of Africa, 1877–1900* (Madison: University of Wisconsin Press, 1982), 184–90.

[7] Ibid., 145–50, 191–94. Williams omits Seme from his list of early students.

[8] P. Olisanwuche Esedebe, *Pan-Africanism: The Idea and the Movement, 1776–1963* (Washington, D.C.: Howard University Press, 1982), 45.

[9] Originally called the Universal Negro Improvement and Conservation Association and African Communities League.

[10] Quoted in E. David Cronon, *Black Moses: Marcus Garvey and the Universal Negro Improvement Association* (Madison: University of Wisconsin Press, 1969), 17.

[11] Ibid., 45, quoting Claude McKay.

[12] Robert A. Hill and Gregory A. Pirio, "'Africa for the Africans': The Garvey Movement in South Africa, 1920–1940," in *The Politics of Race, Class, and Nationalism in Twentieth-Century South Africa*, ed. Shula Marks and Stanley Trapido (London: Longman, 1987), 209–53, and T. O. Ranger, "The Myth of the Afro-American in East Central Africa, 1900–1939," unpublished paper, 1971.

[13] John Hope Franklin, *From Slavery to Freedom: A History of Negro Americans*, 3rd ed. (New York: Alfred A. Knopf, 1967), 401.

[14] Quoted in P. C. Lloyd, *Africa in Social Change* (Hammondsworth, England: Penguin Books, 1967), 276.

[15] Constance Agatha Cummings-John, *Memoirs of a Krio Leader*, ed. La Ray Denzer (Ibadan, Nigeria: Sam Bookman, 1995), 25, 27–29.

[16] Era Bell Thompson, *Africa: Land of My Fathers* (Garden City, N.Y.: Doubleday, 1954), 251, 281.

[17] Ibrahim Sundiata, *Brothers and Strangers: Black Zion, Black Slavery, 1914–1940* (Durham, N.C.: Duke University Press, 2003), 344–45. In comparison, 55 percent of white Americans in 1957 could name no African territory, and 6 percent could name five African territories.

[18] A deeply sensitive and personal account of this issue is Philippe Wamba's *Kinship: A Family Journey in Africa and America* (New York: Plume, 1999). With an African American mother and a Congolese father, Wamba grew up in Africa and America and

was sensitive to the issues and perceptions that divided and united black people. He died in a tragic auto accident in Kenya in 2002 at the age of thirty-one.

[19]United States Office of Immigration Statistics, Yearbook of Immigration Statistics 2004 (www.uscis.gov); Rachel L. Swarns, "'African-American' Becomes a Term for Debate," New York Times, 29 Aug. 2002; Sam Roberts, "More Africans Enter U.S. Than in Days of Slavery," New York Times, 21 Feb. 2005.

# PART TWO

# The Documents

# 1

# Seeking New Homes in Europe and Africa, 1773–1859

## 1

### PHILLIS WHEATLEY

## *On Being Brought from Africa to America*

### *1773*

*Named for the slave ship* Phillis *that brought her from West Africa in 1761 and the family that purchased the frail eight-year-old in Boston, Phillis Wheatley (ca. 1753–1784) accomplished much in her brief life. Though a slave and female, she had the good fortune to receive a good education, which she made good use of when she turned her hand to poetry. In 1773 her talents won her the patronage of the countess of Huntingdon, a patron of many blacks, who brought the twenty-year-old to London and arranged for the publication of a book of her poems, which won favorable reviews. Wheatley was only the second American woman (of any color) to publish a book of poems. The decision in the Somerset case the year before enabled Wheatley to win a promise of manumission from her owners in return for her agreeing to go back to Boston to care for the ailing Mrs. Wheatley. The title of her volume,* Poems on Various Subjects: Religious and Moral, *suggests her preferred subject matter. One of these poems, printed here, expresses the view that she shared with many Atlantic blacks: seeing enslavement as a providential act, with a*

---

Note: Spelling and punctuation in the documents have been made to conform to a single editorial style for consistency.

---

Phillis Wheatley, *Poems on Various Subjects: Religious and Moral* (London, 1773).

*rebuke to those who fail to appreciate that racial equality in God's eyes is a necessary corollary of divine redemption.*

'TWAS mercy brought me from my *Pagan* land,
Taught my benighted soul to understand
That there's a God, that there's a *Saviour* too:
Once I redemption neither sought nor knew.
Some view our sable race with scornful eye,
"Their color is a diabolic die [dye]."
Remember, *Christians*, *Negro[e]s* black as *Cain*,
May be refin'd, and join th' angelic train.

# 2

## OLAUDAH EQUIANO

# Going Back to Africa as a Missionary or Settler

## 1779 and 1786

*Olaudah Equiano (ca. 1745–1797) has become one of the best-known Atlantic blacks of the eighteenth century on the basis of his autobiography, which he first published in 1789 and which has been revised and reprinted numerous times. He bought his way out of slavery and made his living mostly as a seaman traveling to various continents. There is reason to doubt that his account of his early life in Africa is genuine and thus to question the name by which he is now best known. In his adult life he consistently used the name Gustavus Vassa, as he does in this passage from his* Interesting Narrative of the Life of Olaudah Equiano or Gustavus Vassa, the African. *Vassa did not in fact become a missionary and failed in his second attempt to accompany the Sierra Leone immigrants back to Africa. However, he was active in abolitionist causes in Britain, and the proceeds from his books made him perhaps the wealthiest black man in Britain. In 1792 he married a much younger Englishwoman, with whom he had two daughters before his death in 1797.*

The Interesting Narrative of the Life of Olaudah Equiano or Gustavus Vassa, the African, 6th ed. (London, 1793), chap. 12. Courtesy of the Burns Library, Boston College.

In 1779, I served Governor [Matthias] Macnamara, who had been a considerable time on the coast of Africa. In the time of my service, I used to ask frequently other servants to join me in family prayer; but this only excited their mockery. However, the Governor, understanding that I was of a religious turn, wished to know what religion I was of; I told him I was a protestant of the church of England, agreeable to the thirty-nine articles of that church; and that whomsoever I found to preach according to that doctrine, those I would hear. A few days after this, we had some more discourse on the same subject; when he said he would, if I chose, as he thought I might be of service in converting my countrymen to the Gospel faith, get me sent out as missionary to Africa. I at first refused going, and told him how I had been served on a like occasion by some white people the last voyage I went to Jamaica, when I attempted (if it were the will of God) to be the means of converting the Indian prince; and said I supposed they would serve me worse than Alexander, the coppersmith, did St. Paul, if I should attempt to go amongst them in Africa.* He told me not to fear, for he would apply to the Bishop of London to get me ordained.† On these terms I consented to the Governor's proposal, to go to Africa in hope of doing good, if possible, amongst my countrymen; so, in order to have me sent out properly, we immediately wrote the following to the late Bishop of London:

To the Right Reverend Father in God, ROBERT, Lord Bishop of London:
THE MEMORIAL OF GUSTAVUS VASSA
SHEWETH,
That your memorialist is a native of Africa, and has a knowledge of the manners and customs of the inhabitants of that country.

That your memorialist has resided in different parts of Europe for twenty-two years last past, and embraced the Christian faith in the year 1759.

That your memorialist is desirous of returning to Africa as a missionary, if encouraged by your Lordship, in hopes of being able to prevail upon his countrymen to become Christians; and your memorialist is the more induced to undertake the same, from the success that has attended the like undertakings when encouraged by the Portuguese through their different settlements on the Coast of Africa, and also by the Dutch; both governments encouraging the blacks, who, by their education are qualified to undertake the same, and are found more proper than European clergymen, unacquainted with the language and customs of the country.

*1 Timothy 1:18–20, 2 Timothy 4:14.
†Robert Lowth (1710–1787), bishop of London.

Your memorialist's only motive for soliciting the office of a missionary is that he may be a means, under God, of reforming his countrymen and persuading them to embrace the Christian religion. Therefore your memorialist humbly prays your Lordship's encouragement and support in the undertaking.

*GUSTAVUS VASSA*

... [T]he Bishop by the Governor's desire ... received me with much condescension and politeness; but from some certain scruples of delicacy, and saying the Bishops were not of opinion of sending a new missionary to Africa, he declined to ordain me.

My sole motive for thus dwelling on this transaction, or inserting these papers, is the opinion which gentlemen of sense and education, who are acquainted with Africa, entertain of the probability of converting the inhabitants of it to the faith of Jesus Christ, if the attempt were countenanced by the Legislature. ...

On my return to London in August [1786], I was very agreeably surprised to find that the benevolence of government had adopted the plan of some philanthropic individuals, to send the Africans from hence to their native quarter; and that some vessels were then engaged to carry them to Sierra Leone, an act which redounded to the honor of all concerned in its promotion, and filled me with prayers and much rejoicing. There was then in the city a select committee of gentlemen for the black poor, to some of whom I had the honor of being known; and as soon as they heard of my arrival, they sent for me to the committee. When I came there, they informed me of the intention of government; and as they seemed to think me qualified to superintend part of the undertaking, they asked me to go with the black poor to Africa. I pointed out to them many objections to my going; and particularly I expressed some difficulties on the account of the slave dealers, as I would certainly oppose their traffic in human species by every means in my power. However, these objections were over-ruled by the gentlemen of the committee, who prevailed on me to consent to go; and recommended me to the honorable commissioners of his Majesty's Navy, as a proper person to act as commissary for government in the intended expedition; and they accordingly appointed me, in November 1786, to that office, and gave me sufficient power to act for the government, in the capacity of commissary. ...

During my continuance in the employment of government, I was struck with the flagrant abuses committed by the agent, and endeavored to remedy them, but without effect. One instance, among many which I could produce, may serve as a specimen. Government had ordered to be provided all necessaries (slops, as they are called, included) for 750 persons; however, not being able to muster more than 426, I was ordered to send the superfluous slops, &c., to the king's stores at Portsmouth; but, when I demanded them for that purpose from the agent, it appeared they had never been bought, though paid for by government. But that was not all; government were not the only objects of peculation; these poor people suffered infinitely more; their accommodations were most wretched, many of them wanted beds, and many more clothing and other necessaries. For the truth of this, and much more, I do not seek credit from my own assertion. I appeal to the testimony of Captain Thompson, of the *Nautilus*, who convoyed us, to whom I applied in February 1787, for a remedy, when I had remonstrated to the agent in vain, and even brought him to be a witness of the injustice and oppression I complained of. I appeal also to a letter written by these wretched people, so early as the beginning of the preceding January, and published in the *Morning Herald*, on the 4th of that month, signed by twenty of their chiefs.

I could not silently suffer government to be thus cheated, and my countrymen plundered and oppressed, and even left destitute of the necessaries for almost their existence. I therefore informed the Commissioners of the Navy of the agent's proceeding, but my dismission was soon after procured, by means of a gentleman in the city, whom the agent, conscious of his peculation, had deceived by letter, and who, moreover, empowered the same agent to receive on board, at the government expense, a number of persons as passengers, contrary to the orders I received. By this I suffered a considerable loss in my property; however the commissioners were satisfied with my conduct, and wrote to Captain Thompson, expressing their approbation of it.

Thus provided, they proceeded on their voyage; and at last, worn out by treatment, perhaps not the most mild, and wasted by sickness, brought on by want of medicine, clothes, bedding, &c., they reached Sierra Leone, just at the commencement of the rains. At that season of the year, it is impossible to cultivate the lands; their provisions therefore were exhausted before they could derive any benefit from agriculture; and it is not surprising that many, especially the Lascars, whose constitutions are very tender, and who had been cooped up in ships from October to June, and accommodated in the manner I have mentioned, should be so wasted by the confinement as not to survive it.

Thus ended my part of the long talked of expedition to Sierra Leone; an expedition which, however unfortunate in the event, was humane and politic in its design, nor was its failure owing to government; everything was done on their part; but there was evidently sufficient mismanagement attending the conduct and execution of it to defeat its success.

# 3

## OTTOBAH CUGOANO

# An Account of the First Black Emigration from Britain to Sierra Leone

## 1787

*Just as Equiano would do two years later, the Anglo-African John Stewart used an African name, Ottobah Cugoano (ca. 1757–ca. 1803), when in 1787 he published his* Thoughts and Sentiments on the Evil and Wicked Traffic of the Slavery and Commerce of the Human Species, *from which is taken the following account of the problems that beset the first voyage from Britain to Sierra Leone. Cugoano includes an account of his enslavement in West Africa at the age of twelve or thirteen by "some of my own complexion," his experiences in slavery in the West Indies, and his accompanying his master to Britain at the end of 1772. There he sought instruction as a Christian and was active in abolitionist causes. Although he was a less accomplished writer than Equiano, Cugoano's passionate tract against the slave trade made a strong impression. The details of his later life and death are obscure.*

Particular thanks is due to every one of that humane society of worthy and respectful gentlemen, whose liberality hath supported many of the

Ottobah Cugoano, *Thoughts and Sentiments on the Evil and Wicked Traffic of the Slavery and Commerce of the Human Species* (London, 1787), 138–42. Courtesy of O'Neill Library, Boston College.

Black poor of London. . . . The part that the British government has taken, to co-operate with them, has certainly a flattering and laudable appearance of doing some good; and the fitting out ships to supply a company of Black People with clothes and provisions, and to carry them to settle at Sierra Leona, in the West coast of Africa, as a free colony to Great-Britain, in a peaceable alliance with the inhabitants, has every appearance of honor, and the approbation of friends. According to the plan, humanity hath made its appearance in a more honorable way of colonization, than any Christian nation have ever done before, and may be productive of much good, if they continue to encourage and support them. But after all, there is some doubt whether their own flattering expectation in the manner as set forth to them, and the hope of their friends may not be defeated and rendered abortive; and there is some reason to fear, that they never will be settled as intended, in any permanent and peaceable way at Sierra Leona.

This prospect of settling a free colony to Great-Britain in a peaceable alliance with the inhabitant of Africa at Sierra Leona, has neither altogether met with the credulous approbation of the Africans here, nor yet been sought after with any prudent and right plan by the promoters of it. Had a treaty of agreement been first made with the inhabitants of Africa, and the terms and nature of such a settlement been fixed upon, and its situation and boundary pointed out; then might the Africans, and others here, have embarked with a good prospect of enjoying happiness and prosperity themselves, and have gone with a hope of being able to render their services, in return of some advantage to their friends and benefactors of Great-Britain. But as this was not done, and as they were to be hurried away at all events, come of them after[wards] what would; and yet, after all, to be delayed in the ships before they were set out from the coast, until many of them have perished with cold, and other disorders, and several of the most intelligent among them are dead, and others that, in all probability, would have been most useful for them were hindered from going, by means of some disagreeable jealousy of those who were appointed as governors, the great prospect of doing good seems all to be blown away. And so it appeared to some of those who are now gone, and at last, haphazard, were obliged to go; who endeavored in vain to get away by plunging into the water, that they might, if possible wade ashore, as dreading the prospect of their wretched fate, and as beholding their perilous situation, having every prospect of difficulty and surrounding danger.

What with the death of some of the original promoters and proposers of this charitable undertaking, and the death and deprivation of others that were to share the benefit of it, and by the adverse motives of those employed to be the conductors thereof, we think it will be more than what can be well expected, if we ever hear of any good in proportion to so great, well-designed, laudable, and expensive charity. Many more of the Black People still in this colony would have, with great gladness, embraced the opportunity, longing to reach their native land; but as the old saying is, A burnt child dreads the fire, some of these unfortunate sons and daughters of Africa have been severally unlawfully dragged away from their native abodes, under various pretenses, by the insidious treachery of others, and have been brought into the hands of barbarous robbers and pirates, and, like sheep to the market, have been sold into captivity and slavery, and thereby have been deprived of their natural liberty and property, and every connection that they held dear and valuable, and subjected to the cruel service of the hard-hearted brutes called planters. But some of them, by various services either to the public or to individuals, as more particularly in the course of [the] last war, have gotten their liberty again in this free country. They are thankful for the respite, but afraid of being ensnared again; for the European seafaring people in general, who trade to foreign parts, have such a prejudice against Black People, that they use them more like asses than men, so that a Black Man is scarcely ever safe among them. Much assiduity was made use to persuade the Black People in general to embrace the opportunity of going with this company of transports; but the wiser sort declined from all thoughts of it, unless they could hear of some safety. . . . They were afraid that their doom would be to drink of the bitter water. For can it be readily conceived that government would establish a free colony for them nearly on the spot, while it supports its forts and garrisons, to ensnare, merchandise, and to carry others into captivity and slavery.

## 4

## THOMAS PETERS

# A Black Loyalist Petitions
# for a Better Place of Settlement
### 1790

*Born among the Egba Yoruba, Thomas Peters (ca. 1738?–1792) was
kidnapped and enslaved in 1760. Sold away from French Louisiana, he
ended up in 1770 in North Carolina, from where he escaped and joined
the British side early in the American Revolution. He rose to the rank of
sergeant in the British regiment of Guides and Pioneers, also known as
the Black Pioneers. After the British defeat he and his wife and two children were evacuated to Nova Scotia along with other Loyalists, black
and white. There the blacks generally received smaller allotments of
land in less desirable locations than those allocated to white Loyalists.
Moreover, they lacked the money, tools, livestock, and servants that the
whites generally had. Peters and another black sergeant were chosen as
spokesmen for the Pioneers' grievances. When the governor did not correct the problems, Peters was chosen to go to London, where he made
contact with sympathetic Englishmen and, with their help, presented the
following petition to a rising member of the British Cabinet. In the end
many Pioneers decided to emigrate to Sierra Leone and again chose
Peters as one of their leaders. He died a few months after landing in
Freetown.*

The humble Memorial and Petition of Thomas Peters a free Negro
and late a Serjt. in the Regiment of Guides and Pioneers serving in
North America under the Command of Genl. Sir Henry Clinton on
Behalf of himself and others the Black Pioneers and loyal Black
Refugees hereinafter described
Sheweth
 That your Memorialist and the said other Black Pioneers having
served in North America as aforesaid for the Space of seven years and

Great Britain, Public Record Office, Colonial Office file CO217/63fol. 63.

upwards, during the War, afterwards went to Nova Scotia under the Promise of obtaining the usual Grant of Lands and Provision.

That notwithstanding they have made repeated Applications to all Persons in that Country who they conceived likely to put them in Possession of the due Allotments, the said Pioneers with their Wives and Children amounting together in the whole to the Number of 102 People now remain at Annapolis Royal have not yet obtained their Allotments of Land except one single Acre of land each for a Town Lot and tho' a further Proportion of 20 Acres each Private man (viz) about a 5th part of the Allowance of Land that is due to them was actually laid out and located for them agreeable to the Governor's Order it was afterwards taken from them on Pretense that it had been included in some former Grant and they have never yet obtained other Lands in Lieu thereof and remain destitute and helpless.

That besides the said 102 People at Annapolis who have deputed your Memorialist to represent their unhappy Situation there is also a Number of free Black Refugees consisting of about 100 Families or more at New Brunswick in a like unprovided and destitute Condition for tho' some of them have had but a Part of their Allowance of Land offered to them it is so far distant from their Town Lots (being 16 or 18 miles back) as to be entirely useless to them and indeed worthless in itself from its remote situation.

That the said two Descriptions of People having authorized and empowered your Memorialist to act for them as their Attorney he has at much Trouble and Risk made his way into this Country in the Hope that he should be able to procure for himself and his Fellow Sufferers some Establishment where they may attain a competent Settlement for themselves and be enabled by their industrious exertions to become useful subjects to his Majesty.

That some Part however of the said Black People are earnestly desirous of obtaining their due Allotment of Land and remaining in America but others are ready and willing to go wherever the Wisdom of Government may think proper to provide for them as free Subjects of the British Empire.

Your Memorialist therefore (most honble Sir) humbly prays that you will most humanely consider the Case of your Memorialist and the said other Black People and by laying the same before his Majesty or otherwise as you shall deem most proper that they may be afforded such Relief as shall appear to be best adapted to their Circumstances and Situation.

## NANCY GARDNER PRINCE

# Visits to the Russian Court
# in St. Petersburg and to Jamaica

### 1824 and 1840

---

*Born free in Massachusetts, Nancy Gardner Prince (1799–ca. 1856) survived a difficult childhood in which she worked from a young age as a servant. After she married an African American seaman who had taken service in the Russian court, she journeyed with her husband back to St. Petersburg. Decorative Africans had been common in European royal courts for more than a century. She returned to Boston in 1833 shortly before her husband's death and became involved in the abolitionist movement there. In 1840 this activity drew her to visit Jamaica, where the slaves had been emancipated in 1834. In Jamaica she became involved in raising money for missions and orphanages. The following selections are from the account of her life and travels that she published in 1850 — one of the first autobiographies by an African American woman. Two more editions were issued in her lifetime.*

---

Mr. Prince was born in Marlborough, and lived in families in this city. In 1810 he went to Gloucester, and sailed with captain Theodore Stanwood, for Russia. He returned with him, and remained in his family, and at this time visited at my mother's. He sailed with captain Stanwood in 1812, for the last time. The Captain took with him his son Theodore, in order to place him in School in St. Petersburg. When the Captain sailed for home, Mr. Prince went to serve the Princess Purtossof, one of the noble ladies of the Court. The palace where the imperial family reside is called the court, or the seat of Government. This magnificent building is adorned with all the ornaments that possibly can be explained; there are hundreds of people that inhabit it, besides the soldiers that guard it. There are several of these splendid

---

Nancy Prince, *A Narrative of the Life and Travels of Mrs. Nancy Prince*, 2nd ed. (Boston: Published by the Author, 1853), 22–24, 48–49, 51.

edifices in the city and vicinity. The one that I was presented in, was in a village, three miles from the city. After leaving the carriage, we entered the first ward; where the usual salutation by the guards was performed. As we passed through the beautiful hall, a door was opened by two colored men in official dress. The Emperor Alexander, stood on his throne, in his royal apparel. The throne is circular, elevated two steps from the floor, and covered with scarlet velvet, tasseled with gold; as I entered, the Emperor stepped forward with great politeness and condescension, and welcomed me, and asked several questions; he then accompanied us to the Empress Elizabeth; she stood in her dignity, and received me in the same manner the Emperor had. They presented me with a watch, &c. It was customary in those days, when any one married, belonging to the court, to present them with gifts, according to their standard; there was no prejudice against color; there were there all casts, and the people of all nations, each in their place.

The number of colored men that filled this station was twenty; when one dies, the number is immediately made up. Mr. Prince filled the place of one that had died. They serve in turns, four at a time, except on some great occasions, when all are employed. Provision is made for the families within or without the palace. Those without go to court at 8 o'clock in the morning; after breakfasting, they take their station in the halls, for the purpose of opening the doors, at signal given, when the Emperor and Empress pass. . . .

I then called on the American Consul, he told me he was very glad to see me for such a purpose as I had in view in visiting Jamaica, but he said it was a folly for the Americans to come to the island to better their condition; he said they came to him every day praying him to send them home. He likewise mentioned to me the great mortality among the emigrants. The same day I saw the Rev. J. S. Beadslee, one of our missionaries, who wished me to accompany him forty miles into the interior of the country.

On May the 18th, I attended the Baptist Missionary meeting, in Queen Street Chapel; the house was crowded. Several ministers spoke of the importance of sending the gospel to Africa; they complimented the congregation on their liberality the last year, having given one hundred pounds sterling; they hoped this year they would give five hundred pounds, as there were five thousand members at the present time. There was but one colored minister on the platform. It is generally the policy of these missionaries to have the sanction of colored ministers, to all their assessments and taxes. The colored people give more readily, and are less suspicious of imposition, if one from themselves recommends the measure; this the missionaries understand very well, and know how to take advantage of it. On the 22d and 23d of June, the colored Baptists held their missionary meeting, the number of ministers, colored and mulattoes, was 18, the colored magistrates were present. The resolutions that were offered were unanimously accepted, and every thing was done in love and harmony.

. . . There were in the House of Correction three hundred culprits; they are taken from there, to work on plantations. I went to the Admiral's house, where the emigrants find a shelter until they can find employment, then they work and pay for their passage. Many leave their homes and come to Jamaica under the impression that they are to have their passage free, and on reaching the island are to be found [there], until they can provide for themselves.

How the mistake originated, I am not able to say, but on arriving here, strangers poor and unacclimated, find the debt for passage money hard and unexpected. It is remarkable that whether fresh from Africa, or from other islands, from the South or from New England, they all feel deceived on this point. I called on many Americans and found them poor and discontented,—ruing the day they left their country, where, notwithstanding many obstacles, their parents lived and died,—a country they helped to conquer with their toil and blood; now shall their children stray abroad and starve in foreign lands.

# 6

## FREDERICK DOUGLASS

# A Black Man in England Reflects on Racist America

## 1846

*One of the most famous and extraordinary Americans of his day, Frederick Douglass (1818–1895) escaped from slavery to the relative freedom of Massachusetts, where he became active in the abolitionist movement. Despite his limited formal education, he became a spellbinding orator and writer with an extraordinary command of language. His autobiography,*

*The Liberator*, 30 January 1846.

*first published in 1845, was a great success that went through many editions, and was the occasion for his tour of Britain the next year, during which this letter was written to the Massachusetts abolitionist leader William Lloyd Garrison. The letter captures the profound alienation that racial discrimination created, even in the non-slave-holding parts of the United States. Nevertheless, Douglass returned to the United States and devoted himself to the struggle for equal rights. His abolitionist paper, The North Star, published from 1847 in Rochester, New York, also championed women's emancipation, and Douglass was invited to second the motion to give women the vote at the Seneca Falls, New York, Women's Rights Convention in 1848. He fled the United States for a time after John Brown's raid on Harpers Ferry. During the Civil War he was an adviser to President Abraham Lincoln and after the war to President Andrew Johnson. Among his many postwar activities, he served as U.S. federal marshal for the District of Columbia and as the American consul-general to Haiti.*

---

VICTORIA HOTEL, Belfast,
January 1st, 1846

MY DEAR FRIEND GARRISON:

I am now about to take leave of the Emerald Isle, for Glasgow, Scotland. I have been here a little more than four months. Up to this time, I have given no direct expression of the views, feelings, and opinions which I have formed, respecting the character and condition of the people of this land. I have refrained thus purposely. I wish to speak advisedly, and in order to do this, I have waited till I trust experience has brought my opinions to an intelligent maturity. I have been thus careful, not because I think what I may say will have much effect in shaping the opinions of the world, but because whatever of influence I may possess, whether little or much, I wish it to go in the right direction, and according to truth. I hardly need say that, in speaking of Ireland, I shall be influenced by no prejudices in favor of America. I think my circumstances all forbid that. I have no end to serve, no creed to uphold, no government to defend; and as to nation, I belong to none. I have no protection at home, or resting-place abroad. The land of my birth welcomes me to her shores only as a slave, and spurns with contempt the idea of treating me differently. So that I am an outcast from the society of my childhood, and an outlaw in the land of my birth. "I am a stranger with thee, and a sojourner as all my fathers were." That

Frederick Douglass.
Courtesy of the University of
Texas Libraries, the University
of Texas at Austin.

men should be patriotic is to me perfectly natural; and as a philosophical fact, I am able to give it an *intellectual* recognition. But no further
can I go. If ever I had any patriotism, or any capacity for the feeling, it
was whipt out of me long since by the lash of the American soul-
drivers.

In thinking of America, I sometimes find myself admiring her
bright blue sky—her grand old woods—her fertile fields—her beautiful rivers—her mighty lakes, and star-crowned mountains. But my
rapture is soon checked, my joy is soon turned to mourning. When I
remember that all is cursed with the infernal spirit of slaveholding,
robbery, and wrong,—when I remember that with the waters of her
noblest rivers, the tears of my brethren are borne to the ocean, disregarded and forgotten, and that her most fertile fields drink daily of the
warm blood of my outraged sisters, I am filled with unutterable
loathing, and led to reproach myself that any thing could fall from my
lips in praise of such a land. America will not allow her children

to love her. She seems bent on compelling those who would be her warmest friends, to be her worst enemies. May God give her repentance before it is too late, is the ardent prayer of my heart. I will continue to pray, labor, and wait, believing that she cannot always be insensible to the dictates of justice, or deaf to the voice of humanity. . . .

I can truly say, I have spent some of the happiest moments of my life since landing in this country. I seem to have undergone a transformation. I live a new life. The warm and generous co-operation extended to me by the friends of my despised race—the prompt and liberal manner with which the press has rendered me its aid—the glorious enthusiasm with which thousands have flocked to hear the cruel wrongs of my down-trodden and long-enslaved fellow-countrymen portrayed—the deep sympathy for the slave, and the strong abhorrence of the slaveholder, everywhere evinced—the cordiality with which members and ministers of various religious bodies, and of various shades of religious opinion, have embraced me, and lent me their aid—the kind hospitality constantly proffered to me by persons of the highest rank in society—the spirit of freedom that seems to animate all with whom I come in contact—and the entire absence of everything that looked like prejudice against me, on account of the color of my skin—contrasted so strongly with my long and bitter experience in the United States, that I look with wonder and amazement on the transition. In the Southern part of the United States, I was a slave, thought of and spoken of as property. . . . In the Northern States, a fugitive slave, liable to be hunted at any moment like a felon, and to be hurled into the terrible jaws of slavery—doomed by an inveterate prejudice against color to insult and outrage on every hand, (Massachusetts out of the question)—denied the privileges and courtesies common to others in the use of the most humble means of conveyance—shut out from the cabins on steamboats—refused admission to respectable hotels—caricatured, scorned, scoffed, mocked, and maltreated with impunity by any one, (no matter how black his heart,) so he has a white skin. But now behold the change! Eleven days and a half gone, and I have crossed three thousand miles of the perilous deep. Instead of a democratic government, I am under a monarchical government. Instead of the bright blue sky of America, I am covered with the soft grey fog of the Emerald Isle. I breathe, and lo! the chattel becomes a man. I gaze around in vain for one who will question my equal humanity, claim me as his slave, or offer me an insult. I employ a cab—I am seated beside white people—I reach the hotel—I enter the same door—I am shown into the same parlor—I dine at the same table—and no one is offended. No delicate nose grows deformed in my presence. I find no difficulty here in obtaining admission into any place of worship, instruction, or amusement, on equal terms with people as white as any I ever saw in the United States. I meet nothing to remind me of my complexion. I find myself regarded and treated at every turn with the kindness and deference paid to white people. When I go to church, I am met by no upturned nose and scornful lip to tell me, *"We don't allow niggers in here!"*

I remember, about two years ago, there was in Boston, near the southwest corner of Boston Common, a menagerie. I had long desired to see such a collection as I understood were being exhibited there. Never having had an opportunity while a slave, I resolved to seize this, my first, since my escape. I went, and as I approached the entrance to gain admission, I was met and told by the door-keeper, in a harsh and contemptuous tone, *"We don't allow niggers in here."* I also remember attending a revival meeting in the Rev. Henry Jackson's meeting-house, at New-Bedford, and going up the broad aisle to find a seat. I was met by a good deacon, who told me, in a pious tone, *"We don't allow niggers in here!"* Soon after my arrival in New-Bedford from the South, I had a strong desire to attend the Lyceum, but was told, *"They don't allow niggers in here!"* While passing from New York to Boston on the steamer Massachusetts, on the night of 9th Dec. 1843, when chilled almost through with the cold, I went into the cabin to get a little warm. I was soon touched upon the shoulder, and told, *"We don't allow niggers in here!"* On arriving in Boston from an anti-slavery tour, hungry and tired, I went into an eating-house near my friend Mr. Campbell's, to get some refreshments. I was met by a lad in a white apron, *"We don't allow niggers in here!"* A week or two before leaving the United States, I had a meeting appointed at Weymouth, the home of that glorious band of true abolitionists, the Weston family, and others. On attempting to take a seat in the Omnibus to that place, I was told by the driver, (and I never shall forget his fiendish hate,) *"I don't allow niggers in here!"* Thank heaven for the respite I now enjoy! I had been in Dublin but a few days, when a gentleman of great respectability kindly offered to conduct me through all the public buildings of that beautiful city; and a little afterwards, I found myself dining with the Lord Mayor of Dublin. What a pity there was not some American democratic Christian at the door of his splendid mansion, to bark out at my approach, *"They don't allow niggers in here!"* The truth is, the people here know nothing of the republican negro hate prevalent in our glorious land. They measure and esteem men according to their moral and intellectual worth, and not according to the color of their skin. Whatever may be said of the aristocracies here, there is none based on the color of a man's skin. This species of aristocracy belongs pre-eminently to "the land of the free, and the home of the brave." I have never found it abroad, in any but Americans. It sticks to them wherever they go. They find it almost as hard to get rid of it as to get rid of their skins.

The second day after my arrival at Liverpool, ... I went to Eaton Hall, the residence of the Marquis of Westminster, one of the most splendid buildings in England. On approaching the door, I found several of our American passengers, who came out with us in the Cambria, waiting at the door for admission, as but one party was allowed in the house at a time. We all had to wait till the company within came out. And of all the faces, expressive of chagrin, those of the Americans were pre-eminent. They looked as sour as vinegar, and bitter as gall, when they found I was to be admitted on equal terms with themselves. When the door was opened, I walked in, on an equal footing with my white fellow-citizens, and from all I could see, I had as much attention paid me by the servants that showed us through the house, as any with a paler skin. As I walked through the building, the statuary did not fall down, the pictures did not leap from their places, the doors did not refuse to open, and the servants did not say, *"We don't allow niggers in here!"*

<br>

# 7

# AMERICAN COLONIZATION SOCIETY

## Annual Report

### 1850

*Established in 1816, the American Colonization Society (ACS) sponsored voyages to send free African Americans to Africa. Its supporters were an odd mixture of well-meaning white philanthropists, clergy, and abolitionists genuinely concerned with improving the welfare of blacks,*

*Thirty-Third Annual Report of the American Colonization Society with the Proceedings of the Board of Directors, and of the Society at Its Annual Meeting, January 15, 1850* (Washington, D.C.: C. Alexander, 1850), 8–11.

*and southern slave owners, seeking to rid the United States of the dangerous example of freepersons of African descent in the wake of the successful slave uprising in Haiti. The society's funds came from the sale of membership certificates and from state and federal grants. In 1822 it founded the colony of Liberia, whose territories were gradually expanded. Early settlement ventures were disastrous due to deadly diseases such as yellow fever and to the poor preparation of the black colonists for the rigors of a tropical environment. The 1850 meeting at which the annual report was made was presided over by Henry Clay (1777–1852), a powerful southern politician who was a founder of the ACS and its longtime president.*

---

We have made arrangements for the departure of three expeditions within the next forty days. The Liberia Packet will sail from Norfolk, Va., on the 26th inst. We have 224 applicants for a passage in her, but shall send only about 160. A vessel will sail from Savannah, Geo., on the 14th February, with about 200 emigrants, and a vessel from New Orleans, the 26th February, with about 100.

It is very embarrassing, with our present empty treasury, and large debt, to be compelled to send out so many emigrants, so early in the year. But circumstances over which we could exert no control have rendered it important, if not indispensable, that these people should all go at the times appointed. Not to send them, would be ruinous to their prospects, and disastrous to our hopes of future usefulness. In obedience, therefore, to the resolution of the Board of Directors at their last annual meeting, we have agreed to send them, relying upon our auxiliary Societies, and a liberal and sympathizing public for the means of defraying the expenses.

Among the encouraging events of the past year, we number the continued increase of applicants for emigration to Liberia. We think the fact is fully established that there will always be more persons desirous of, and needing, the aid of the Society, than it will be able to assist. . . .

In the history of the Republic of Liberia, the past year, there is much to awaken gratitude, and give encouragement for future and enlarged operations. Several new tracts of territory have been purchased, and treaties of peace and friendship made with the surrounding tribes. The slave trade at New Cesters has been entirely broken up, and at Gallinas it has been for the present stopped, with every prospect of its final extinction. To accomplish this object, President

Roberts assures us in his last dispatch, nothing is wanting but the means of purchasing the coast lying between the northern boundary of Liberia and the southern boundary of Sierra Leone. The legacy of the late John Hoff, of Philadelphia, if we can receive it, together with the distinguished liberality of a gentleman in Cincinnati, and one in England, will very nearly, if not quite, make up the amount required.

The man-of-war, presented to the Republic by Great Britain, has proved a valuable acquisition, and rendered essential service to the commerce and welfare of Liberia. The income from duties and other sources, has been on the increase, and promises to be sufficient for all the expenses of the government. Considerable embarrassment, however, has been felt in consequence of the heavy debt, about $6,000, incurred in fitting out the military expedition against the slave factory at New Cesters. Great credit is due to the men who planned and executed that undertaking.

The chief want of Liberia at present is an increased population of intelligent and industrious citizens, and enlarged resources for the support of schools, and the execution of internal improvements. On this point, it is pleasant to know that much interest is felt both in this country and in Liberia; and that measures are in progress to render them important assistance. . . .

In conclusion, we earnestly, affectionately, and importunately invoke the philanthropic every where to continue, and increase their generosity to our cause! We are able to show diligence on our part, in prosecuting the enterprise, and frugality in the use of all the pecuniary means placed at our disposal. The expenditure of the funds contributed by private benevolence has purchased, on a benighted coast, a territory of more than four hundred miles in extent, has chartered ships, transported to the home and continent of their fathers, 6,653 of our free people of color, who have formed, and are capable of maintaining a prosperous and independent government; has brought under the canopy of Liberian law more than 80,000 hitherto wild and untutored savages, has abolished the slave trade for several hundred miles on the coast, has founded schools, churches, and printing presses, has cleared farms and sprinkled abroad the green tints of agriculture, has established the temples of justice, transplanted our beautiful arts to a distant continent, and carried our mother tongue to where it will become the language of millions for ages to come; and above all, and by means of all, established the institutions of our holy religion in a land hitherto shrouded in the deepest heathenish darkness! LIBERIA is a Republic reared by private benevolence. It demonstrates what may

be done with adequate means at command. The work is now compara-
tively easy. The experiment has been made. The true policy has been
discovered, and all the preliminaries settled. The means and appliances are well understood. The business is reduced to such a perfect
system, that every mite now contributed can be made to achieve
direct results to its utmost possible capacity. We therefore call upon all
to strengthen our hands and encourage our hearts, for the work of a
century yet remains to be done. Liberia needs more of our people,
that she may send her influence eventually into the heart of Africa.
They are anxious to go, and shall we forbid them to cherish the hope
that they may one day plant their feet on the soil which once their
fathers trod! The claims of humanity and the commands of the Most
High summon us to redoubled zeal and activity! The time has come
when the resources of the Society must be greatly enlarged, or it must
falter in the work which is demanded of it.

# 8

## MARTIN R. DELANY

# Changing Views of the Wisdom
# of African American Emigration

## *1859*

*Born to free black parents in Virginia, Martin R. Delany (1812–1885)
was one of the most accomplished African Americans of his time. He distinguished himself as a Harvard-educated doctor, orator, writer, explorer,
army officer, and ardent black nationalist. Like many African American
leaders in the United States, Delany was initially deeply opposed to black
emigration, but his views altered under the rising disabilities created by
the Fugitive Slave Law of 1850, which caused him to question his ability
to be loyal to an America where blacks were neither free nor citizens. He
led an expedition to the Niger in 1859, where he sought to find a home
among Africans unsullied by colonialism. Although his emigration plans*

M. R. Delany, *Official Report of the Niger Valley Exploring Party* (New York: T. Hamilton, 1861), 70, 74–75, 104–5, 110–11.

*produced no tangible results, his enthusiasm for a pristine Africa contrasts with the stern condemnation of some missionaries and prefigures the sometimes romantic vision of Africa of later generations of blacks outside Africa.*

The whole face of the country extending through the Aku region or Yoruba, as it is laid down on the large missionary map of Africa, is most beautifully diversified with plains, hills, dales, mountains, and valleys, interlined with numerous streams, some of which are merely temporary or great drains; whilst the greater part are perennial, and more or less irrigating the whole year, supplying well the numerous stocks of cattle and horses with which that country is so well everywhere provided. The climate is most delightful. . . .

The people are of fine physical structure and anatomical conformation, well and regularly featured; not varying more in this particular from the best specimen of their own race than the Caucasian or Anglo-Saxon from that of theirs. They are very polite—their language abounding in vowels, and consequently euphonious and agreeable—affable, sociable, and tractable, seeking information with readiness, and evincing willingness to be taught. They are shrewd, intelligent, and industrious, with high conceptions of the Supreme Being, only using their images generally as mediators. "So soon," said an intelligent missionary, "as you can convince them that there is a mediator to whom you *may talk, but cannot see,* just as soon can you make Christians of them"; their idea being that God is too great to be directly approached; therefore there must be a mediator to whom they must talk that they can see, when God will listen and answer if pleased. . . .

Wherever there are missionaries, there are schools both Sabbath and secular, and the arts and sciences, and manners and customs, more or less of civilized life, are imparted. I have not as yet visited a missionary station in any part of Africa, where there were not some, and frequently many natives, both adult and children, who could speak, read, and write English, as well as read their own language; as all of them, whether Episcopalian, Wesleyan, Baptist, or Presbyterian, in the Yoruba country, have Crowther's editions of religious and secular books in the schools and churches, and all have native agents, interpreters, teachers (assistants), and catechists or readers in the mission. These facts prove indisputably great progress; and I here take much pleasure in recording them in testimony of those faithful laborers in that distant vineyard of our heavenly Father in my fatherland. Both male and female missionaries, all seemed much devoted to their work, and anxiously desirous of doing more. Indeed, the very fact of there being as many native missionaries as there are now to be found holding responsible positions, as elders, deacons, preachers, and priests, among whom there are many finely educated, and several of them authors of works, not only in their own but the English language . . . all show that there is an advancement for these people beyond the point to which missionary duty can carry them. . . .

It is clear, then, that essential to the success of civilization, is the establishment of all those social relations and organizations, without which enlightened communities cannot exist. To be successful, these must be carried out by proper agencies, and these agencies must be a *new element* introduced into their midst, possessing all the attainments, socially and politically, morally and religiously, adequate to so important an end. This element must be *homogenous* in all the *natural* characteristics, claims, sentiments, and sympathies—the *descendants of Africa* being the only element that can effect it. To this end, then, a part of the most enlightened of that race in America design to carry out these most desirable measures by the establishment of social and industrial settlements among them, in order at once to introduce, in an effective manner, all the well-regulated pursuits of civilized life.

That no mis-step be taken and fatal error committed at the commencement, we have determined that the persons to compose this new element to be introduced into Africa, shall be well and most carefully selected in regard to moral integrity, intelligence, acquired attainments, fitness, adaptation, and, as far as practicable, religious sentiments and professions. We are serious in this; and, so far as we are concerned as an individual, it shall be restricted to the letter, and we will most strenuously oppose and set our face against any attempt from any quarter to infringe upon this arrangement and design. Africa is our fatherland and we its legitimate descendants, and we will never agree nor consent to see this—the first voluntary step that has ever been taken for her regeneration by her own descendants—blasted by a disinterested or renegade set, whose only object might be in the one case to get rid of a portion of the colored population, and in the other, make money, though it be done upon the destruction of every hope entertained and measure introduced for the accomplishment of this great and prospectively glorious undertaking. We cannot and will not permit or agree that the result of years of labor and anxiety shall be blasted at one reckless blow, by those who have never spent a day in the cause of our race, or know nothing about our wants and requirements. The descendants of

Africa in North America will doubtless, by the census of 1860, reach five millions; those of Africa may number two hundred millions. I have outgrown, long since, the boundaries of North America, and with them have also outgrown the boundaries of their claims. I, therefore, cannot consent to sacrifice the prospects of two hundred millions, that a fraction of five millions may be benefitted, especially since the measures adopted for the many must necessarily benefit the few.

Africa, to become regenerated, must have a national character, and her position among the existing nations of the earth will depend mainly upon the high standard she may gain compared with them in all her relations, morally, religiously, socially, politically, and commercially.

# 2

# Missions to Redeem Africa, 1853–1891

## 9

### ALEXANDER CRUMMELL

## *Hope for Africa*

### *1853*

*Born in New York City to a West African father and an African American mother, Alexander Crummell (1819–1898) overcame the obstacles placed in the way of black students, attending a Protestant Episcopal seminary in Boston and earning a B.A. from Cambridge University in England in 1853. Already an ordained priest, he spent the next twenty years as a missionary and educator. From 1873 he was an influential pastor in Washington, D.C., where he was active in the black community and among African American clergymen. A man of great learning, Dr. Crummell was also a skilled writer and orator. In addition to* Africa and America *(1891), he also wrote* The Future of Africa *(1862), a collection of speeches, sermons, and essays from which the following selection is taken. In it he contemplates Africa's changing future in light of recent events from a deep and broad historical perspective.*

The Negro race is to be found in every quarter of the globe. Stolen from their homes, and reduced to abject vassalage, they are gathered together by thousands and tens of thousands, and even millions, in

Alexander Crummell, *The Future of Africa, Being Addresses, Sermons, Etc., Etc., Delivered in the Republic of Liberia* (New York: Charles Scribner, 1862), 289–92, 294–95, 297, 300–301.

lands separated, by thousands of miles, from the primitive seat of their ancestors, and the rude hamlets of their sires.

Now it is with respect to the Negro race, as thus scattered abroad through the world, as well as dwelling in their homes in Africa, that I shall apply my text: my purpose is to show that, in the merciful providence of God, the Negro race is fast approaching the day of complete evangelization. . . .

In the *first* place, I am to refer you to secular evidences—to some temporal providences, that are alike recent and remarkable; which show that the day of the regeneration of Africa and her children is fast drawing nigh.

We stand now, my hearers, in the central period of the present century: we are living in the year of grace eighteen hundred and fifty-three. Now just go back with me to the commencement of this century, and look at this race of which we are speaking. What then meets our eyes? Why we find one universal fact connected with the Negro race—the fact of universal slavery, and the slave trade. If we turned to the West Indies, whether under Danish, Spanish, Dutch, or English rule, the black man, everywhere, was a chattel. If we turned to the American continent, we would have found the race in the same position there, whether under the Protestant rule of the North American colonies, or under the Romish[1] rule of the South American States. If we turned to Africa herself, we would have seen the whole extent of that vast continent given to the spoiler, robbed of her children—the vast interior converted into a hunting-ground for capturing miserable and wretched human beings;—drenched on every side with fraternal blood;—and the long line of the coast, for thousands of miles, evidencing, at every point, how prolific was the slave trade, in woes and agonies and murders, by the bleached bones, or the bloody tracks of its countless victims!

And what was the *status* of the Negro race at this time, in either Europe or America? It is one of the sad results of crime that its deadly influences strike down deep into every part of the human constitution: it both dementates and demoralizes men. The slave trade not only lowered the nations that engaged in it, in the scale of humanity, and in the tone of their morals, but it robbed them of the clearness of their mental vision. They not only robbed the Negro of his freedom—they added another crime thereto: they denied his humanity. Yes, at the commencement of this century it was a debated question among culti-

[1]Catholic. [Ed.]

vated, thoughtful, nay even scientific minds, whether the Negro was indeed an integral member of the human species.

This, then, was the condition of the Negro race fifty years ago—this the estimation in which that race was held.

And now I desire to call your attention to the great change which has taken place in both these respects, since that period.

Since the commencement of this century, the leading European and American Governments have renounced all participation in that nefarious traffic which has barbarized Africa; and some of them have declared the slave trade piracy. The black man, thus held in a state of servitude, has been emancipated. The cheerful voice of freedom has been heard all around the islands of the Caribbean Sea; and eight hundred thousand human beings, under British rule, have been awakened by its grateful tones, to liberty and manhood. Influenced by this gracious example, France has stricken the shackle and the fetter from the limbs of three hundred thousand men and women. And Denmark has given the promise that she too will follow, at an early day, in the same benevolent pathway.

In America, the civil condition of the Negro race presents, in many places, the same signs of a half century's progress. From Mexico, Bolivia, Peru, Colombia, and Guatemala, the signs and tokens of Negro slavery were obliterated long before the system was abolished in your own western possessions. And although it still exists in Brazil, in the United States, and in Cuba, we have nevertheless some few signs of advancement, some evident indications that it must ere long yield and come to an end: for the commerce of the world is against slavery; the free-trade principle of the age is against it; science in her various developments is against it; the literature of the day is just now being brought to bear, in a most marvellous manner, against it; and the free sentiments of the world are against it, and doom it to an early utter oblivion!

Turning again to the coast of Africa we meet with most cheerful evidence of progress. Along a coast extending some two thousand five hundred miles in length, the slave trade has been entirely uprooted and destroyed; and from more than three-fourths of the strongholds once occupied by the traders, they have been driven out, never more to return. Along this region—including some of the richest and most productive portions of the African continent—legitimate trade has sprung up; and instead of a revolting commerce in the bodies and souls of men, and women, and even babes, we see industrious communities springing up, civilization introduced, and a trade commenced which already has swelled up, in exports alone to Europe and America, to more than two millions of pounds per annum.

Besides these various evidences of the progress of my race during the last half century, I must not fail to notice one striking fact: that is, that within this period, the black government of HAYTI has come into existence; the African colony of SIERRA LEONE has been established — a colony which has already become the cradle of missions, the mother of churches, the parent of colonies. And, moreover, we see now rising with, we trust, hopeful indications, on the western coast of Africa, the lone star of the black REPUBLIC OF LIBERIA.

And still another movement of a similar character is now projected by Englishmen, from your own West India Islands: a movement of brightest promise, even while yet in the bud; which contains within its folds the germs of a new African nationality of a civilized and Christian type. In the island of Barbadoes a society has been formed, under the patronage of the Governor, the Bishop, and other chief personages, whose object is to transplant colonies of black men from the West Indies to the coast of Africa. The black population have become interested, and have formed societies, and declare their strong spiritual yearnings for Africa. They are to go in communities with clergymen, physicians, mechanics, and laborers, and form themselves at once into organized settlements. An agent has been in this country seeking funds for the foundation of a college. An important society has been formed in England, under the patronage of the Archbishop of Canterbury, and the leading dignitaries of the Church, and great statesmen. Already two African youths are under a system of instruction for missionary usefulness. . . .

The contrast I have just presented between the commencement of this century and the present moment, holds in an equal degree with respect to the spiritual condition of this race, as to their civil and political status.

Prior to the commencement of this century, the Negro race had been left in a state of almost absolute spiritual neglect. Along the whole line of the west coast of Africa, not a mission had been commenced to evangelize nations; not a spire pointed its silent finger, with a heavenly significancy, to the skies. The masses of the black population of America and the West Indies were in a state of heathenism, though surrounded by the Christian institutions of the whites. Both custom and law forbade the instruction of Negroes, and superadded fear prevented the formation of schools. Nay, more than this: the conquerors of the black race were as yet undecided whether their bondmen were capable of spiritual illumination, or were heirs of immortality. . . .

And now, when we turn to Africa, how great the change! How wonderful and pleasing the contrast! "Previous to the year 1832, there was not a mission anywhere between Sierra Leone and the Cape of Good Hope." Now, "during the last fifteen or sixteen years"—I use the words of another—"there have been established as many as twelve independent missions, at the distance of 100 or 200 miles from each other, embracing three times that number of outstations along the coast, and a still greater number of outstations interiorward." To hundreds of thousands of the nations, on the coast and in the interior, the Gospel of glad tidings is regularly preached. Its life-giving power is manifested in the marked revolution which is going on in their tastes and habits, and in the change of their customs. Christian communities are being gathered together; civilized and Christian institutions are formed, and are extending themselves. Christianity has made itself felt in the family, in the domestic relations of life, in trade, in law, in the "modus operandi" of their Governments. Thousands of children are now regularly receiving instruction in our holy religion, and the enlightenment which comes from mental training. Already one high-school has furnished a score and more of catechists and teachers; has produced three native young men, fit candidates for holy orders in the Church, who are preaching the Gospel to their own kith and kin in heathen darkness. This same school—the Fourah Bay Institution—has now a dozen young men fit candidates for holy orders; and another set of youths trained in the languages and in science, also preparing for sacred duties and the ministerial call. At another place on the coast, two other high schools are already in operation; two colleges, one on a large scale, are projected, and will soon commence operations. Indeed, so great, so increasing, and so important are the spiritual interests of the nations, that the Episcopal Church of America is now strengthening all its posts on the coast of Africa; and, to use the words of its Foreign Secretary, in a letter to myself, she expects that the Church there, that is in Liberia, will soon be permanently established; and last year she commissioned a Bishop to head her movements in the mission there, in the Republic of Liberia. And since the consecration of Bishop Payne, the mother Church of England has met the needs and the demands of your own missions and African colonies by the consecration of the Bishop of Sierra Leone.

## 10

## EDWARD WILMOT BLYDEN

# An Appeal for Black Emigration to Liberia

### 1887

*Born in the Danish West Indies before they were bought by the United States, Edward Wilmot Blyden (1832–1912) was deeply committed from his youth to black equality and Christian evangelization. Denied entry to a theological school in the United States in 1850 because of his race, he chose to emigrate to Liberia, where he finished high school and was soon the school's principal. Blyden was also ordained in the Presbyterian Church. In 1862 the linguistic prodigy was appointed professor of classics (Latin and Greek) at the new Liberia College, where he introduced the study of Arabic. He served Liberia abroad in several diplomatic capacities, held different cabinet posts, and ran an unsuccessful campaign for president of the republic. Blyden also taught in Sierra Leone in the early twentieth century. This selection captures something of his views on Liberia.*

An European writer, delighting in epigrammatic rhetoric, has recently said, "The eighteenth century stole the black man from his country; the nineteenth century steals his country from the black man." And, just as the stealing of the man in the eighteenth century originated in philanthropic ideas, so the motive for stealing his country in the nineteenth century is put into philanthropic language. The nations engaged in the "scramble" are all models of the highest civilization, and their aims and purposes are all in the interest of enlightenment and progress. The Congo Conference laid down admirable rules for occupation and protectorates, whatever the native may have to say against them. But they will not countenance any acts against right and justice. They are at once the invaders of his country and the protectors of his rights. The spirit of the international alliance is the spirit of liberty and equity for Africa.

Edward Wilmot Blyden, *Christianity, Islam, and the Negro Race*, 2nd ed. (London: W. B. Wittingham, 1888), 383–85, 405, 430–32.

But it does not seem probable to us that what foreigners have failed to accomplish in all the past ages will be achieved by their descendants of this generation. Modern Europe, with all its vast machinery of intellectual and material progress, and with all its humanitarian intentions—with all its appliances for civilizing, instructing, and elevating—stands paralyzed before difficulties not a whit less appalling than those which, for centuries, have confronted European efforts in this country....

The Negro, in exile, is the only man, born out of Africa, who can live and work and reproduce himself in this country. His residence in America has conferred upon him numerous advantages. It has quickened him in the direction of progress. It has predisposed him in favor of civilization, and given him a knowledge of revealed truth in its highest and purest form. We believe that the deportation of the Negro to the New World was as much decreed by an all-wise Providence, as the expatriation of the Pilgrims from Europe to America. When we say that Providence decreed the means of Africa's enlightenment, we do not say that He decreed the wickedness of the instruments. When the deportation first began, it was looked upon as simply the transportation of Africans to America for purposes of labor; but with a view, also, as Sir John Hawkins made Queen Elizabeth believe, to their spiritual improvement. But, in course of time, human passions became mixed up with, and wicked hands prosecuted, what it had been before determined should be carried out; and the enterprise, having, at first, a beneficent aim and a humane form, became the slave trade, with all its unspeakable enormities....

After this survey of the European in Africa, and the African in America, it is difficult to escape the conclusion forced upon Bishop Haven, after visiting Liberia, that the solution of Africa in America, is America in Africa; and further, that the solution of Africa in Africa, is Africa in America. This brings us to a consideration of the work and its results, of the only agency which is laboring to bring about the solution by the means just suggested, namely, the *American Colonization Society....*

The methods generally pursued, apart from the principle of the Liberian enterprise, will never cause Christianity to penetrate the interior with any hope of bringing the tribes under its sway. Of another thing I am not much less assured, that Mohammedanism—unless Liberia is strengthened and stimulated by an increase of civilized population and schools—will extend its influence to the sea along the whole of Upper Guinea, and will control the indigenous tribes. This it will do with the countenance and support of European governments, dependent for their revenues upon a trade largely under the control of the sober and energetic Moslems.

The religion of Arabia has the advantage of numbers in its work in Africa. The religion of America may also have this advantage, if the Church there will get near enough to the unsophisticated Negro to understand his broken utterances about Africa. . . .

Bishop Taylor has recognized this important fact, and he is endeavoring to demonstrate the feasibility and necessity of *colonies* for the greater and ultimate success of mission work in Africa. He has recently wisely adopted Liberia as a base and strategic point for his operations, where, protected in his rear by a regular government in sympathy with his work, he will not be subject to the intrusion of the many conflicting influences to which he is exposed in the Congo country.

# 11

## HENRY McNEAL TURNER

# An African American Bishop's Views of the Evangelization of Africa

## 1891

*A free native of South Carolina, Henry McNeal Turner (1834–1915) was ordained in 1853 and was briefly the first black chaplain in the United States Army. After the Civil War he turned to politics, helping organize the Georgia Republican Party and serving briefly in the Georgia legislature. An author, educator, and civil rights activist, he was one of the most prominent and ardent advocates of the back-to-Africa movement and regularly proclaimed, "God is black." In 1880 he became the twelfth bishop of the African Methodist Episcopal (AME) Church. In that capacity he attempted with some success to spread the AME Church in Liberia, Sierra Leone, and southern Africa. The selection*

H. M. Turner, *African Letters* (Nashville: Publishing House A.M.E. Sunday School Union, 1893), 72–74.

*reflects his thoughtful and critical approach to settlement and understanding Africans.*

I have left Monrovia and am now some seventy-five miles up the Sherbro River, interior-ward from the ocean. The native towns and vast population of our people living on each side of this river, and all through the bush, is simply wonderful. As you ascend the Sherbro, every now and then, small inlets can be seen flowing in from the land, while trees lock their branches across them, and flower-bearing vines festoon them with garlands of fragrant drapery. But, reverberating through and under these over-arched inlets, you can hear the voices of scores of natives, as they chant their rowing songs; for the native Africans sing as they work, especially as they row their boats, till they burst from under the green sceneries with small canoes laden with all kinds of fruit. Often a Mohammedan priest sits in front, gorgeously robed, as though he was on watch for whisky; as the sixty millions of Mohammedans in Africa hate whisky as they do the devil himself. Say what you please about the Mohammedans and their plurality of wives (which of course no Christian can endorse), I verily believe that God is holding these Mohammedans intact, and that they will serve as the forerunners of evangelical Christianity; in short, that the Mohammedan religion is the morning-star to the sun of pure Christianity. I have not spoken on any occasion against liquor-drinking in Africa but some Mohammedan has come and shaken my hand after service, and thanked me for fighting whisky. One thanked me "for cursing liquor," and said, "Our church and religion all curse it, too; it be our greatest foe." God save the Mohammedans, is my prayer, till the Christian Church is ready to do her whole duty. Beyond the fact that the Mohammedans allow more than one wife, they are as upright in conduct and civil behavior as any people in the land.

I regret to say what I am now going to write, but I promised to do it, and I suppose I had better keep my word.

The leading men, or a large number of them in Liberia, are disgusted with a majority of the representatives that our government sends over here. They say if our government cannot find sober, cool-headed, dignified, and intelligent representatives of our own color to send here, ask the president to send white men. Dr. Henry Highland Garnett is the only man sent here, whom all join in complimenting, for many years. They say Dr. Garnett was a gentleman and a diplomat of high order. They also speak kindly of Hon. Alexander Clark, so far as his sobriety and morality are concerned, but say that he had no knowledge of diplomacy. Some of our representatives have so far ignored the rules of diplomatic dignity or decorum that they have tried to force themselves into the President's Cabinet meetings. But I will tell no more, as I dislike gossip in any form; yet they prefer a white man to some of our colored men whom the presidents have sent here.

It appears that the American minister is the Dean of the Diplomatic Corps at Monrovia, and in any formal meeting or reception he is the presiding officer, as he ranks the representatives of all other nations; therefore he should be a model man in every respect.

Liberia, as I have said before, is a most beautiful country, and nature has supplied it with all that heart could wish. I never wanted to be a young man so badly in my life. I would come here, and, if I had half as much sense as I have now, I would be worth a fortune in ten years. Nevertheless, as I have said before, I would advise no one to come here without a hundred or two dollars. This is not the place for any one to come without money. Well, if he is a mechanic, viz., carpenter, blacksmith, painter, tailor, watchmaker, or professional, as a doctor or a lawyer, he might do well enough; but a mere laborer should bring some money, for the native African stands ready, ten thousand strong, to snatch up all the mere common labor to be done, at twenty-five cents per day, or five dollars a month; and two native Africans can do more hard work in one day than five of our ordinary men, such is their strength and vigor.

As for the acclimating process, nearly everybody must pass through it, yet all do not have the fever. Men, and women too, who have been here ten and fifteen years, tell me they have never had anything like fever. But if a person comes here, young or old, with any chronic disease lurking in his system, Africa is apt to purge it out, or kill the person in the process of purgation. At all events, the party will get better or worse. But if a person comes here healthy, sound, and sober, there is no more danger than in any other change of climate.

One thing the black man has here—that is, manhood, freedom, and the fullest liberty; he feels as a lord, and walks and talks the same way.

I notice when the English, or even the cultured Africans, speak of the colored people coming here from America or elsewhere they do not use the terms "emigrate," or "African emigration," as we do in America; but, instead, they invariably say, "repatriate," or use the term, the "repatriation of the black man," or, as some say, the "negro"; nor are the terms "emigrate" or "immigrate" used, even among the common people, as they say, "coming home," or "When are you all coming home?" The native African, from the kings down, cannot realize that the black man in America is at home across the sea.

**12**

**SAMUEL AJAYI CROWTHER**

## An African Bishop Directs Christian Evangelization in Africa

*1869*

---

*Enslaved when Muslim African invaders overran his town in 1821, the young Ajayi (ca. 1806–1891) was sold into the Atlantic slave trade. A British patrol intercepted his ship and liberated the prisoners in Sierra Leone, where, under the influence of English missionaries, Ajayi was educated and received his new names when he accepted Christianity. The bright lad was devoted to education and religion, becoming the first student at the Christian Institution (later called Fourah Bay College). Following further education in London, he chose ordination in the Church of England in 1843. He was among the first Protestant missionaries to his native Yoruba homeland and went on two explorations of the lower Niger River in search of further mission outposts. In 1864 Crowther was consecrated as a bishop and placed in charge of all the Anglican missions along the lower Niger. While never wavering in his devotion to the truth and value of Christianity and Western education, he also used his special talents to translate prayers and scriptures into African languages, translating parts of the Bible into Yoruba and compiling religious materials in other African languages. In the following selections Crowther expresses his views on missionary endeavors in Africa. His reflections on the phrase "Africa for the Africans" may in part connect with Delany's use of that phrase.*

---

The first selection is from Jesse Page, *The Black Bishop: Samuel Adjai Crowther* (London: Hodder and Stoughton, 1908), 307–8, and the second from J. F. Ade Ajayi, *Christian Missions in Nigeria, 1841–1891: The Making of a New Elite* (Evanston, Ill.: Northwestern University Press, 1965), 224.

If it were possible to go out now in the simple character and spirit of the primitive missionaries and preach the Gospel, "providing neither gold, nor silver, or brass in our purses," etc., on the principle of faith that God will provide our daily food, shall we find the men among ourselves ready to go out in the name of Christ and do so? . . . No one can desire our self-support and independent action more than the Mother Church, whose offspring we are. The timid and anxious trial she is now and then making by a gradual withdrawal of foreign influence, by leaving the superintendence of entire parishes and training schools to the native agents which now constitute the native protectorate, is a clear evidence that no one would rejoice more than she to see the largest portion of West Africa entirely worked by African pastors and missionaries on a self-supporting system if they are so circumstanced as to be able to do so. . . . The small spots occupied as mission stations on the line of the coast, at great distances of some hundreds of miles apart, which are touched at by Royal Mail steamers, do not constitute the whole continent of Africa to be evangelized. These places are mere ports, occupied only as starting points to work the main continent teeming with population, of the immense number of which we have no correct idea until we actually enter among them.

What has been done to evangelize the one hundred tribes represented by liberated Africans in the colony of Sierra Leone, such as the kingdoms of Ashantee, Dohomey, Yoruba, Benin, Nupé, Hausa, Bornu, and Ibo on this part of the continent? By the side of one of these kingdoms all the spots occupied on the line of the coast put together will appear as a very little speck, without saying a word of those on the north, south, and east of the continent. "Africa for the Africans," the rest of the world for the rest of mankind! Can the idea thus expressed and widely circulated be applied to the evangelization of Africa? If so, and it be adopted as a watchword, let us raise up and be doing. The land is before us; let us enter the length and the breadth of it and bring the nations to Christ. "Now is the accepted time, now is the day of salvation." If we delay, thousands on thousands will continue to pass away into eternity without the knowledge of Christ, without hope, and without God in the world. Woe be unto us if we preach not unto them the Gospel of salvation in due time! . . .

When we think of the wealth and the advanced civilization and enlightenment of Europe, Asia, and America—three great quarters of the globe—when we reflect that, notwithstanding their great advancement, yet Christians from one quarter go into the others to evangelize the heathen portions of these quarters, when we consider the vast population of China and India—both wealthy and skilful in the arts and sciences, and yet into these countries Christian missionaries are sent by scores from other nations to evangelize the heathen, and their help is hailed with inexpressible joy by the sons of the soil—is it not an act of great ignorance, not to say unpardonable selfishness, on the part of any man to claim "Africa for the Africans alone," when she is neither wealthy, skilful, nor enlightened, to the exclusion of others from other quarters of the globe? Africa has neither knowledge nor skill to devise plans to bring out her vast resources for her own improvement, and, from want of Christian enlightenment, cruelty and barbarity overspread the land to an incredible degree. Therefore to claim "Africa for the Africans alone" is to claim for her the right of continued ignorance to practice cruelty and acts of barbarity as her perpetual inheritance. For it is certain, unless help came from without, a nation can never rise much beyond its present state. "Hath a nation changed their gods which are yet no gods?" No, "for all people will walk every one in the name of God."

[Christianity] has come into the world to abolish and supersede all false religions, to direct mankind to the only way of obtaining peace and reconciliation with their offended God. . . . But it should be borne in mind that Christianity does not undertake to destroy national assimilation; where there are any degrading and superstitious defects, it corrects them; where they are connected with politics, such corrections should be introduced with due caution and with all meekness of wisdom, that there may be good and perfect understanding between us and the powers that be that while we render unto all their dues, we may regard it our bounden duty to stand firm in rendering to God the things that are God's.

Their native Mutual Aid Clubs should not be despised, but where there is any with superstitious connections, it should be corrected and improved after a Christian model. Amusements are acknowledged on all hands to tend to relieve the mind and sharpen the intellect. If any such is not immoral or indecent, tending to corrupt the mind, but merely an innocent play for amusement, it should not be checked because of its being native and of a heathen origin. Of these kinds of amusements are fables, story-telling, proverbs, and songs which may be regarded as stores of their national education in which they exercise their power of thinking: such will be improved upon and enriched from foreign stocks as civilization advances. Their religious terms and ceremonies should be carefully observed; the wrong use made of such terms does not depreciate their real value, but renders them more valid when we adopt them in expressing Scriptural terms in their right senses and places from which they have been misapplied for want of better knowledge.

## 13

### GEORGE WASHINGTON WILLIAMS

# A Report on the Congo Free State to President Benjamin Harrison

## 1890

*Born free in Pennsylvania, George Washington Williams (1849–1891) served in the Union army in the Civil War, in the Mexican army, and again in the U.S. Army fighting Plains Indians. Although he appears to have been semiliterate at this point in his life, he proved to be a brilliant student after he left the military in 1867 and studied briefly at Howard University and in a longer program at Newton Theological Institution in Massachusetts, from which he graduated in 1874. He emerged from his studies with a firm command of spoken and written English and a commitment to the uplifting of black people. He quickly moved on from being a pastor in Boston, founding a black-oriented newspaper in the District of Columbia that soon ceased publication; then, retraining himself in law, he was elected to the Ohio legislature in 1879, the first African American to be a member. In the early 1880s he published the massive two-volume* History of the Negro Race in America from 1619 to 1880, *which started with a review of the history of African kingdoms. Before Williams's early death, he threw himself into the physical and spiritual redemption of Africa. At first he envisioned King Leopold II of Belgium's Congo Free State as a place where that mission could be furthered, but, as is evident in this letter to U.S. president Benjamin Harrison, he became a harsh critic of that deeply flawed colonial venture.*

*A Report upon the Congo-State and Country to the President of the Republic of the United States of America*, 14 Oct. 1890, reprinted in John Hope Franklin, *George Washington Williams: A Biography* (Chicago: University of Chicago Press, 1985), 265–79.

George Washington
Williams, June 1891.
From the National Archives.

Permit me, at this point, to make a statement personal to my-self, but not irrelevant to this Report. I was among the very first of public men in America to espouse the cause of *l'Association Internationale du Congo*. I wrote a series of articles on African geography, during the winter of 1883–1884, in which I combated Portugal's claim to the Congo. In April 1884, I presented an argument before the Senate Committee on Foreign Relations, urging the passage of a resolution recognizing the flag of *l'Association Internationale du Congo*, as the flag of a friendly Government. The resolution passed on the 10th of April, and on the 22nd the Secretary of State, the Honorable FREDERICK J. FRELINGHUYSEN, sent an order instructing the officers of the army and navy of the Republic to salute the flag of *l'Association Internationale du Congo* as the flag of a friendly Government.

Shortly after this I went to Belgium to place before the King certain plans for the perfection of the labor-system in the Congo; and they met the approbation both of the King and HENRY M. STANLEY. On the 21st of August 1889, I published an elaborate historical paper on the Congo; and a few weeks later, at the reunion of the *Anti-Slavery Leaders* at Boston, I offered a resolution, requesting the President of the Republic of the United States to accept the invitation of the King of the Belgians to be represented in an Anti-Slavery-Conference of the Powers of Europe, to unify action upon the land and sea looking towards the abatement of the slave-trade, around and upon the African Continent. Within a few days a representative was appointed, and I sailed for Europe to do whatever I could to promote the success of this notable Conference. I remained at Brussels two months.

Thus much to prove how deeply I have been interested in the success of the Congo State, the overthrow of the African Slave-Power, and the spread of civilization. I have never entertained any other than friendly feelings towards the King of the Belgians and his African State; and my report deals only with those matters *which have come under my personal observation*, or the truth of which has been established by the testimony of competent and veracious witnesses.

The establishment of a State in the Valley of the Congo is due to His Majesty Leopold II, King of the Belgians. On the 13th and 14th days of September 1876, he convened at his Palace at Brussels, a company of distinguished African travellers who represented Germany, Austria-Hungary, France, England, Italy, Russia, and Belgium. The object of this Conference was to devise the best means of opening the Congo-country to commerce and civilization. On the 20th and 21st days of June 1877, another meeting was held at Brussels, when the Conference took definite shape, and *l'Association Internationale du Congo* was formed under the Presidency of the King of the Belgians. He employed HENRY M. STANLEY as his Chief-Agent to proceed to the Congo and secure the country as His Majesty's personal possession. Mr. STANLEY was supposed to have made treaties with more than four hundred native Kings and Chiefs, by which they surrendered their rights to the soil. And yet many of these people declare that they never made a treaty with STANLEY, or any other white man; that their lands have been taken from them by force, and that they suffer the greatest wrongs at the hands of the Belgians. I have never met a chief or tribe or native, man, woman, or child, from Banana, the mouth of the Congo River, to Stanley-Falls at its headwaters, who expressed any other sentiment towards the Congo State than that of hatred, deeply rooted in an abiding sense of injury, injustice, and oppression. In Russia, Crete, and Ireland the constituted authorities have some support from among the people; but in the Congo State there is not one solitary native who would put out his hand to aid the Congo State Government.

Although the majority of the treaties alleged to have been made by Mr. STANLEY, were only witnessed by his servantboy "Dualla," they were accepted as genuine in Europe and America. Having possessed itself of a vast tract of land in the Congo, *l'Association Internationale du Congo*, of which the King of the Belgians was President and treasurer, now sought to obtain recognition in Europe. Failing to secure the countenance of a single Power, the *Association* appealed to the Republic of the United States of America. Its representative was the Hon. HENRY S. SANFORD, a citizen of the United States, who had resided in Belgium for twenty-five or thirty years. Mr. SANFORD had been many years in the diplomatic service, and was well qualified for this delicate mission. He was fortunate to find at Washington a President who was the son of a Baptist clergyman, whose fame chiefly arose from his extreme anti-slavery sentiments and work for the slave in ante-bellum days. Moreover, the Secretary of State was the son of one of the earliest and most eminent of the Presidents of the American Colonization Society. Mr. SANFORD'S course was plain, he appealed to American sentiment and commercial interest; and . . . the flag of the *Association* was recognized. . . .

A small portion of the country, claimed by the *Independent State of Congo*, is divided into Military Districts; the rest is *dominated* by natives whose lawful possession it is. . . .

Each one of these military districts is commanded by an officer of the Belgian Army, supported by other officers and non-commissioned officers. The "Commissaire of District" is of one of three classes, and needs not always be an army officer, for he deals with civil affairs only. All disputes and native *palavers* are settled by the military commander, and sometimes by the commissaire of the district, and their decision is final. When an offense has been committed against the State, the native may be fined, imprisoned, or enslaved. In the Upper-Congo the State officials generally demand slaves for settling native palavers. They promise to liberate these people after seven years service. As far as I have been able to investigate, this system of Government is unjust, capricious, and absolutely cruel. There is scarcely one percent of the State officials, military and civil, who know the native language; and frequently the interpreter, an uneducated negro from Zanzibar or the East-Coast, knows little French, and puts questions indistinctly, or translates the testimony of the natives indifferently. I have seen this in the Supreme Court at Boma also. I called the attention of the Clerk of the Court to the poor French of the Interpreter, and he told me that, if that were all, it would not be so bad; but that the fellow was a *notorious liar* into the bargain! And yet upon this stammering patois hangs the bondage or liberty, the peace and property of many a native.

In addition to these military districts there are more than fifty (50) posts of from two to ten black soldiers in the Upper-Congo. They have no white commissioned officer, and act to suit their own fancy. They receive no supplies from the State, and are expected to levy tribute upon the natives. They seize fish, goats, fowls, eggs, vegetables &c. for their nourishment; and when the natives demur or refuse to be "spoiled," these black pirates burn their villages and confiscate their property. I have been an unwilling and mournful witness to these atrocities. It is almost impossible for a traveller to buy food, [on] account [of] the ravages committed by these buccaneers of the State of Congo, who are guilty of murder, arson, and robbery. Often the natives move their towns miles away rather than submit to the indignities inflicted by an unfeeling mercenary soldiery.

The entire military force of the State of Congo is less than three-thousand (3,000) men, and hundred of miles of the country is without a single soldier. In this country, destitute of a military police and semblance of constituted authority, the most revolting crimes are committed by the natives. They practice the most barbarous religious and funeral rites; they torture, murder, and eat each other. Against these shocking crimes the State puts forth no effort; indeed it systematically abandons thousands of victims to the slaughter every year. Human hands and feet and limbs, smoked and dried, are offered and exposed for sale in many of the native village markets.

From the mouth of the Loumami-River to Stanley-Falls there are thirteen armed Arab camps; and in them I have seen many skulls of murdered slaves pendant from poles and over these camps floating their blood-red flag. I saw nowhere the Congo-State flag, and I know that it would be torn down if it were displayed among these ivory and slave raiders. Here the State has no authority, can redress no wrong, protect no life or property. . . .

The State recruits its soldiers and employs its laborers on the East and West-coast of Africa. . . .

The soldiers serve three years, the workmen one year; and the loss by desertion, sickness, death, and reshipment is about £12,000 = $60,000 per annum. The natives of the Congo serve in the transport corps because there are no Belgians to cruelly treat them; but they will not enter the service of the State. Kindness, firmness, and justice to the natives would soon secure a large and reliable native labor force. But violence and injustice drive these poor children of nature away from the white man. Emigration cannot be invited to the Congo for a quarter of a century, and then only educated blacks from the Southern United States, who have health, courage, morals, and means. They must come only in small companies, not as laborers, but as landed proprietors. One hundred families in ten years would be quite enough and not for twenty five years yet. *White labor can never hope to get a foot-hold here.* . . .

But the State not only suffers the trade in slaves to continue, *it buys the slaves of natives*, and pays to its military officers £3-/- per capita for every able-bodied slave he procures. Every military post in the Upper-Congo thus becomes a slave-market; the native is encouraged to sell slaves by the State, which is always ready to buy them. This buying of slaves is called "redemption," and it is said that after seven years the slave may have his liberty. But it is my opinion that these hapless creatures are the perpetual slaves of the State of Congo.

After thirteen years of occupation by the International Association and State of Congo, no map has been made of the Upper-Congo River; no school has been erected; no hospital founded and nothing contributed to science or geography. At first the Government was international in character, but of late years it has degenerated into a narrow Belgian Colony, *with a determined purpose to drive all other nations out of the Congo that are now represented by trade*. In a letter of instructions to the representative of the Government of the Republic of the United States at Berlin, the Secretary of State wrote on the 17th of October 1884: "As far as the administration of the Congo-Valley is concerned, this Government has shown its preference for a neutral control, such as is promised by the Free-States of the Congo, the nucleus of which has been already created through the organized efforts of the International Association. Whether the approaching Conference can give further shape and scope to this project of creating a great State in the heart of Western Africa, whose organization and administration shall afford a guarantee that it is to be held for all time, as it were, in trust for the benefit of all peoples, remains to be seen." . . .

There is one ray of hope for the Congo, and that is in the character of the Christian Missions.

No foreign missionary field was ever so quickly occupied by Christian workers as the Congo. The American Baptist Missionary Union has eight stations, the English Baptists seven, and the Congo Bololo Mission three; Catholic missions three, one just abandoned, which made four, three Bishop-Taylor-missions, one "faithcure," "Simpson mission," two Swedish missions, twenty-seven (27) in all. Some of them are eminently useful, and several of them are conspic[u]ously helpless. The missionaries have great influence with the natives, and they go and come among the fiercest cannibalistic tribes without fear of being molested. Whenever the friends at home, who support and regulate these missions, will add an industrial feature to each one of them, their efficiency will be increased tenfold.

My travels extended from the mouth of the Congo at Banana, where it empties into the South Atlantic, to its headwaters at the Seventh Cataract, at Stanley-Falls; and from Brazzaville, on Stanley-Pool, to the South Atlantic Ocean at Loango, I passed through the French-Congo, via Comba, Bouenza, and Loudima. In four months, or in one hundred and twenty-five days I travelled 3,266 miles, passing from Southwestern Africa to East Central Africa, and back to the sea. I camped in the bushes seventy-six times, and on other occasions received hospitality of traders, missionaries, and natives. Of my eighty-five natives I lost not a life, although we sometimes suffered from fatigue, hunger, and heat.

Although America has no commercial interests in the Congo it was the Government of the Republic of the United States which introduced this African Government into the sisterhood of States. It was the American Republic which stood sponsor to this young State, which has disappointed the most glowing hopes of its most ardent friends and most zealous promoters. Whatever the Government of the Republic of the United States did for the Independent State of Congo, was inspired and guided by noble and unselfish motives. And whatever it refrains from doing, will be on account of its elevated sentiments of humanity, and its sense of the sacredness of agreements and compacts, in their letter and spirit. The people of the United States of America have a just right to know *the truth*, the *whole truth*, and *nothing but the truth*, respecting the Independent State of Congo, an absolute monarchy, an oppressive and cruel Government, an exclusive Belgian colony, now tottering to its fall. I indulge the hope that when a new Government shall rise upon the ruins of the old, it will be simple, not complicated; local, not European; international, not national; just, not cruel; and, casting its shield alike over black and white, trader and missionary, endure for centuries.

# 3

# The Quest for Unity, Liberation, and Advancement, 1897–1958

## 14

### JOSEPH BOOTH AND JOHN CHILEMBWE

# A Plan for African and African American Cooperation

## 1897

*After a visit to the United States in 1895, Joseph Booth (1851–1932), an Englishman who had worked as a Baptist missionary in southern Africa, became intent on forging an African Christian Union that would unite new African Christians and African Americans in a common struggle for justice and equality. A young African Christian convert, John Chilembwe (?–1915), attached himself to Booth as a servant, interpreter, and protégé. Early in 1897 Chilembwe joined Booth and others in issuing the following mission statement for an African Christian Union that would use African American help in creating mission training schools (Industrial Missions) for Africans and foster African American settlement in Africa. The plan is interesting historically in that it combined Booker T. Washington's idea of practical training for self-sufficiency and the plans later voiced by Marcus Garvey (see Document 18) for black shipping companies. Accompanying Booth to the United States in 1897, Chilembwe completed his theological education in Virginia and was ordained. From 1900 he was active in his own Providence Industrial Mission (with some support from African American Baptists) in*

Joseph Booth, *Africa for the African* (1897), 49–51.

*Nyasaland (as Malawi was then called). Increasingly bothered by European settlers' ill treatment of African laborers and by the British conscription of Africans for service in World War I, Chilembwe began organizing an uprising to drive the whites out or to die trying. The rebellion reached a peak in January 1915, when he and his followers attacked a number of white settlers, killing some of them. Authorities quickly crushed the rebellion. Chilembwe was killed and his mission largely destroyed.*

---

Objects of the Society:

1. To unite together in the name of Jesus Christ such persons as desire to see full justice done to the African race and are resolved to work towards and pray for the day when the African people shall become an African Christian Nation.

2. To provide capital to equip and develop Industrial Mission Stations worked by competent Native Christians or others of the African race; such stations to be placed on a self-supporting and self-propagating basis.

3. To steadfastly demand by Christian and lawful methods the equal recognition of the African and those having blood relationship, to the rights and privileges accorded to Europeans.

4. To call upon every man, woman, and child of the African race, as far as may be practicable, to take part in the redemption of Africa during this generation, by gift, loan, or personal service.

5. To specially call upon the Afro-American Christians, and those of the West Indies to join hearts and hands in the work either by coming in person to take an active part or by generous, systematic contributions.

6. To solicit funds in Great Britain, America, and Australia for the purpose of restoring at their own wish carefully selected Christian Negro families, or adults of either sex, back to their fatherland in pursuance of the objects of the Union; and to organize an adequate propaganda to compass the work.

7. To apply such funds in equal parts to the founding of Industrial Mission centers and to the establishing of Christian Negro settlements.

9.* To firmly, judiciously, and repeatedly place on record by voice

---

*In the original text, the eighth paragraph is numbered "9."

and pen for the information of the uninformed, the great wrongs inflicted upon the African race in the past and in the present, and to urge upon those who wish to be clear of African blood in the day of God's judgements, to make restitution for the wrongs of the past and to withstand the appropriation of the African's land in the present.

10. To initiate or develop the culture of Tea, Coffee, Cocoa, Sugar, etc. etc., and to establish profitable mining or other industries or manufacturers.

11. To establish such transport agencies by land, river, lakes, or ocean as shall give the African free access to the different parts of his great country and people, and to the general commerce of the world.

12. To engage qualified persons to train and teach African learners any department of Commercial, Engineering, nautical, professional, or other necessary knowledge.

13. To mold and guide the labor of Africa's millions into channels that shall develop the vast God-given wealth of Africa for the uplifting and commonwealth of the people, rather than for the aggrandizement of a few already rich persons.

14. To promote the formation of Companies on a Christian basis devoted to special aspects of the work; whose liability shall be limited, whose shares shall not be transferable without the society's consent; whose shareholders shall receive a moderate rate of interest only; whose profits shall permanently become the property of the Trustees of the African Christian Union, for the prosecution of the defined objects of the Union.

15. To petition the government of the United States of America to make a substantial monetary grant to each adult Afro-American desiring to be restored to African soil, as some recognition of the 250 years of unpaid slave labor and the violent abduction of millions of Africans from their native land.

16. To petition the British and other European governments holding or claiming African territory to generously restore the same to the African people or at least to make adequate inalienable native reserve lands, such reserves to be convenient to the locality of the different tribes.

17. To petition the British and other European governments occupying portions of Africa to make substantial and free grants of land to expatriated Africans or their descendents desiring restoration to their fatherland, such grants to be made inalienable from the African race.

18. To provide for all representatives, officials, or agents of the Union and its auxiliaries, inclusive of the Companies it may promote

modest, economical, yet efficient and as far as may be, equable, maintenance, together with due provision for periods of sickness, incapacity, widowhood, or orphanage.

19. To print and publish literature in the interests of the African race and to furnish periodical accounts of the transactions of the Society and its auxiliary agencies, the same to be certified by recognized auditors and to be open to the fullest scrutiny of the Union's supporters.

20. To vest all funds, properties, products, or other sources of income in the hands of Trustees, not less than seven in number, to be held in perpetuity in the distinct interest of the African race and for the accomplishment of the objects herein set forth in 21 clauses.

21. Finally, to pursue steadily and unswervingly the policy:

"AFRICA FOR THE AFRICAN"
and look for and hasten by prayer and united effort the
forming of a united
AFRICAN CHRISTIAN NATION
By God's power and blessing and in His own time and way.
[Signed]                    JOSEPH BOOTH,
English missionary.
JOHN CHILEMBWE,
Ajawa Christian Native.


# 15

## PAMBANI JEREMIAH MZIMBA

## *An African Appeal for African American Help*

### *1901*

*Born in the Cape Colony, P. J. Mzimba (1850–1911) had the good fortune to attend the Lovedale Institution, operated by the United Free Church of Scotland for the education of Africans. He was ordained a minister in that church in 1875, but Rev. Mzimba broke with the white missionaries and founded an independent Presbyterian Church of Africa,*

Pambani Jeremiah Mzimba to BTW, 23 Mar. 1901, printed in *The Booker T. Washington Papers*, vol. 6, *1901–2*, ed. Louis R. Hanlan and Raymond W. Smock (Urbana: University of Illinois Press, 1977), 63.

*which by 1911 had more than thirteen thousand members in thirty-three*
*congregations and a number of schools. This letter, written to Booker T.*
*Washington, shows the growing unanimity of leaders on both sides of the*
*Atlantic who believed that blacks needed to create their own successful*
*institutions to overcome racial prejudice. Five students attended*
*Tuskegee Institute from South Africa in 1902–1903, but it is not clear if*
*they were from Mzimba's church.*

Sir   I have heard very imperfectly of your most important Institute
for the education and improvement of colored young men & young
women who desire to better their condition but have not the means
financially to pay for college training. Your Institute meets such by giving such young men to help themselves by learning a trade and
receive good education as well.

In South Africa there are many young people who are anxious for
education but have not means to pay for college training but who
would be thankful to learn a trade and be able to receive higher education as well. We would be much obliged to you, if you could [write]
fully and even to the smallest particulars about your noble Institution's
[training] and the conditions which would be required from such
young men or women. The sons of Africa are crying to the Africans in
America "Come over & help us." We have about 12 young men & 6
young women anxious to go at once.

# 16

## W. E. B. DU BOIS

# A Critical Assessment of Booker T. Washington

## 1901

*One of the most famous and accomplished African Americans of his day,*
*William Edward Burghardt Du Bois (1868–1963) was born in Great*
*Barrington, Massachusetts, and earned a B.A., M.A., and Ph.D. from*
*Harvard University, where he was a student from 1886 to 1895. He*

W. E. B. Du Bois, *The Souls of Black Folk* (Chicago: 1903), 30–33, 36–37, 38–39.

*cofounded the movement that became the National Association for the Advancement of Colored People (NAACP) and edited the NAACP's influential magazine* Crisis *from 1910 to 1934. He taught economics and history at Atlanta University from 1897 to 1910 and from 1934 to 1944. Besides his active involvement in the civil rights movement in the United States, Du Bois had a longtime interest in Africa. He was active in the Pan-Africanist movement for several decades and spent the last two years of his life in the newly independent republic of Ghana, where he is buried. He was a prolific writer of essays and books, from his pioneering* The Souls of Black Folk *(1903) to his autobiography, which appeared posthumously in 1968. Defying the usual trajectory, Du Bois's politics grew more radical as he aged. He joined the Communist party when he was in his nineties. In this selection from early in Du Bois's career, he takes issue with the leading African American spokesman of the day.*

---

Easily the most striking thing in the history of the American Negro since 1876 is the ascendancy of Mr. Booker T. Washington. It began at the time when war memories and ideals were rapidly passing; a day of astonishing commercial development was dawning; a sense of doubt and hesitation overtook the freedmen's sons,—then it was that his leading began. Mr. Washington came, with a simple definite programme, at the psychological moment when the nation was a little ashamed of having bestowed so much sentiment on Negroes, and was concentrating its energies on Dollars. His programme of industrial education, conciliation of the South, and submission and silence as to civil and political rights, was not wholly original; the Free Negroes from 1830 up to wartime had striven to build industrial schools, and the American Missionary Association had from the first taught various trades; and [Joseph C.] Price and others had sought a way of honorable alliance with the best of the Southerners. But Mr. Washington first indissolubly linked these things; he put enthusiasm, unlimited energy, and perfect faith into this programme, and changed it from a by-path into a veritable Way of Life. And the tale of the methods by which he did this is a fascinating study of human life.

It startled the nation to hear a Negro advocating such a programme after many decades of bitter complaint; it startled and won the applause of the South, it interested and won the admiration of the North; and after a confused murmur of protest, it silenced if it did not convert the Negroes themselves.

To gain the sympathy and cooperation of the various elements comprising the white South was Mr. Washington's first task; and this, at the time Tuskegee was founded, seemed, for a black man, well-nigh impossible. And yet ten years later it was done in the word spoken at Atlanta: "In all things purely social we can be as separate as the five fingers, and yet one as the hand in all things essential to mutual progress." This "Atlanta Compromise" is by all odds the most notable thing in Mr. Washington's career. The South interpreted it in different ways: the radicals received it as a complete surrender of the demand for civil and political equality; the conservatives, as a generously conceived working basis for mutual understanding. So both approved it, and to-day its author is certainly the most distinguished Southerner since Jefferson Davis, and the one with the largest personal following.

Next to this achievement comes Mr. Washington's work in gaining place and consideration in the North. Others less shrewd and tactful had formerly essayed to sit on these two stools and had fallen between them; but as Mr. Washington knew the heart of the South from birth and training, so by singular insight he intuitively grasped the spirit of the age which was dominating the North. And so thoroughly did he learn the speech and thought of triumphant commercialism, and the ideals of material prosperity, that the picture of a lone black boy poring over a French grammar amid the weeds and dirt of a neglected home soon seemed to him the acme of absurdities. One wonders what Socrates and St. Francis of Assisi would say to this.

And yet this very singleness of vision and thorough oneness with his age is a mark of the successful man. It is as though Nature must needs make men narrow in order to give them force. So Mr. Washington's cult has gained unquestioning followers, his work has wonderfully prospered, his friends are legion, and his enemies are confounded. To-day he stands as the one recognized spokesman of his ten million fellows, and one of the most notable figures in a nation of seventy millions. One hesitates, therefore, to criticize a life which, beginning with so little, has done so much. And yet the time is come when one may speak in all sincerity and utter courtesy of the mistakes and shortcomings of Mr. Washington's career, as well as of his triumphs, without being thought captious or envious, and without forgetting that it is easier to do ill than well in the world.

The criticism that has hitherto met Mr. Washington has not always been of this broad character. In the South especially has he had to walk warily to avoid the harshest judgments—and naturally so, for he is dealing with the one subject of deepest sensitiveness to that section. Twice—once when at the Chicago celebration of the Spanish-American War he alluded to the color-prejudice that is "eating away the vitals of the South," and once when he dined with President [Theodore] Roosevelt—has the resulting Southern criticism been violent enough to threaten seriously his popularity. In the North the feeling has several times forced itself into words, that Mr. Washington's counsels of submission overlooked certain elements of true manhood, and that his educational programme was unnecessarily narrow. Usually, however, such criticism has not found open expression, although, too, the spiritual sons of the Abolitionists have not been prepared to acknowledge that the schools founded before Tuskegee, by men of broad ideals and self-sacrificing spirit, were wholly failures or worthy of ridicule. While, then, criticism has not failed to follow Mr. Washington, yet the prevailing public opinion of the land has been but too willing to deliver the solution of a wearisome problem into his hands, and say, "If that is all you and your race ask, take it."

Among his own people, however, Mr. Washington has encountered the strongest and most lasting opposition, amounting at times to bitterness, and even to-day continuing strong and insistent even though largely silenced in outward expression by the public opinion of the nation. Some of this opposition is, of course, mere envy; the disappointment of displaced demagogues and the spite of narrow minds. But aside from this, there is among educated and thoughtful colored men in all parts of the land a feeling of deep regret, sorrow, and apprehension at the wide currency and ascendancy which some of Mr. Washington's theories have gained. These same men admire his sincerity of purpose, and are willing to forgive much to honest endeavor which is doing something worth the doing. They cooperate with Mr. Washington as far as they conscientiously can; and, indeed, it is no ordinary tribute to this man's tact and power that, steering as he must between so many diverse interests and opinions, he so largely retains the respect of all. . . .

Nearly all the former . . . leaders . . . had sought to lead their own people alone, and were usually, save Douglass, little known outside their race. But Booker T. Washington arose as essentially the leader not of one race but of two,—a compromiser between the South, the North, and the Negro. Naturally the Negroes resented, at first bitterly, signs of compromise which surrendered their civil and political rights, even though this was to be exchanged for larger chances of economic development. The rich and dominating North, however, was not only weary of the race problem, but was investing largely in Southern enterprises, and welcomed any method of peaceful cooperation. Thus, by national opinion, the Negroes began to recognize Mr. Washington's leadership; and the voice of criticism was hushed.

Mr. Washington represents in Negro thought the old attitude of adjustment and submission; but adjustment at such a peculiar time as to make his programme unique. This is an age of unusual economic development, and Mr. Washington's programme naturally takes an economic cast, becoming a gospel of Work and Money to such an extent as apparently almost completely to overshadow the higher aims of life. Moreover, this is an age when the more advanced races are coming in closer contact with the less developed races, and the race-feeling is therefore intensified; and Mr. Washington's programme practically accepts the alleged inferiority of the Negro races. Again, in our own land, the reaction from the sentiment of war time has given impetus to race-prejudice against Negroes, and Mr. Washington with-draws many of the high demands of Negroes as men and American citizens. In other periods of intensified prejudice all the Negro's ten-dency to self-assertion has been called forth; at this period a policy of submission is advocated. In the history of nearly all other races and peoples the doctrine preached at such crises has been that manly self-respect is worth more than lands and houses, and that a people who voluntarily surrender such respect, or cease striving for it, are not worth civilizing.

In answer to this, it has been claimed that the Negro can survive only through submission. Mr. Washington distinctly asks that black people give up, at least for the present, three things,—

First, political power,

Second, insistence on civil rights,

Third, higher education of Negro youth,—and concentrate all their energies on industrial education, the accumulation of wealth, and the conciliation of the South. This policy has been courageously and insis-tently advocated for over fifteen years, and has been triumphant for perhaps ten years. As a result of this tender of the palm-branch, what has been the return? In these years there have occurred:

1. The disfranchisement of the Negro.

2. The legal creation of a distinct status of civil inferiority for the Negro.

3. The steady withdrawal of aid from institutions for the higher training of the Negro.

These movements are not, to be sure, direct results of Mr. Wash-ington's teachings; but his propaganda has, without a shadow of doubt, helped their speedier accomplishment. The question then comes: Is it possible, and probable, that nine millions of men can make effective progress in economic lines if they are deprived of political rights, made a servile caste, and allowed only the most meagre chance for developing their exceptional men? If history and reason give any distinct answer to these questions, it is an emphatic *No*. . . .

The other class of Negroes who cannot agree with Mr. Washington has hitherto said little aloud. They deprecate the sight of scattered counsels, of internal disagreement; and especially they dislike making their just criticism of a useful and earnest man an excuse for a general discharge of venom from small-minded opponents. Nevertheless, the questions involved are so fundamental and serious that it is difficult to see how men like the Grimkes, Kelly Miller, J. W. E. Bowen, and other representatives of this group, can much longer be silent. Such men feel in conscience bound to ask of this nation three things:

1. The right to vote.
2. Civic equality.
3. The education of youth according to ability.

They acknowledge Mr. Washington's invaluable service in counselling patience and courtesy in such demands; they do not ask that ignorant black men vote when ignorant whites are debarred, or that any reasonable restrictions in the suffrage should not be applied; they know that the low social level of the mass of the race is responsible for much discrimination against it, but they also know, and the nation knows, that relentless color-prejudice is more often a cause than a result of the Negro's degradation; they seek the abatement of this relic of barbarism, and not its systematic encouragement and pampering by all agencies of social power from the Associated Press to the Church of Christ. They advocate, with Mr. Washington, a broad system of Negro common schools supplemented by thorough industrial training; but they are surprised that a man of Mr. Washington's insight cannot see that no such educational system ever has rested or can rest on any other basis than that of the well-equipped college and university, and they insist that there is a demand for a few such institutions throughout the South to train the best of the Negro youth as teachers, professional men, and leaders.

This group of men honor Mr. Washington for his attitude of conciliation toward the white South; they accept the "Atlanta Compromise" in its broadest interpretation; they recognize, with him, many signs of promise, many men of high purpose and fair judgment, in this section; they know that no easy task has been laid upon a region already tottering under heavy burdens. But, nevertheless, they insist that the way to truth and right lies in straightforward honesty, not in indiscriminate flattery; in praising those of the South who do well and criticizing uncompromisingly those who do ill; in taking advantage of the opportunities at hand and urging their fellows to do the same, but at the same time in remembering that only a firm adherence to their higher ideals and aspirations will ever keep those ideals within the realm of possibility.

# 17

## PIXLEY KA ISAKA SEME

# An African Lawyer Urges Black South Africans to Unite
## 1911

*Born in the British colony of Natal (from 1910 a part of South Africa), Pixley ka Isaka Seme (1881–1951) attended an American Congregationalist mission school, whose teachers arranged to send him for further education to Mount Hermon School in Massachusetts. After contemplating possible careers as a missionary and a physician, Seme earned a B.A. from Columbia University in 1906 and went on to earn a law degree at Oxford University in 1909. In 1910 he returned to the newly unified South Africa, where he practiced law in Johannesburg and was active in African political activities. He was one of the founding members and first treasurer of the pivotal nationalist organization, the African National Congress (ANC), in 1912. (The first ANC president was John L. Dube, his cousin, who had helped pay Seme's school fees.) In 1928 Columbia University bestowed an honorary doctor of laws degree on the successful lawyer. Seme subsequently served as president of the ANC from 1930 to 1937. He married a daughter of the king of Swaziland, one of his clients. The selection shows the efforts under way in South Africa for African unity; these efforts have interesting parallels to movements in black America.*

Pixley ka Isaka Seme, "Native Union," *Imvo Zabantsundu*, 24 Oct. 1911.

There is today among all races and men a general desire for progress, and for co-operation, because co-operation will facilitate and secure that progress. This spirit is due no doubt to the great triumph of Christianity which teaches men everywhere that in this world they have a common duty to perform both towards God and towards one another. It is natural, therefore, that there should arise even within and among us this striving, this self-conscious movement, and sighing for Union. We are the last among all the nations of the earth to discover the priceless jewels of co-operation, and for this reason the great gifts of civilization are least known among us today. I repeat, co-operation is the key and the watchword, which opens the door, the everlasting door, which leads into progress and all national success. The greatest success shall come when man shall have learned to co-operate, not only with his own kith and kin but also with all peoples and with all life.

The South African Native Congress is the voice in the wilderness bidding all the dark races of this sub-continent to come together once or twice a year in order to review the past and reject therein all those things which have retarded our progress, the things which poison the springs of our national life and virtue; to label and distinguish the sins of civilization, and as members of one house-hold to talk and think loudly on our home problems and the solution of them.

Such national Conferences of the people are bound to give a wide publication of the Natives' own views on the questions which primarily concern him to-morrow and today. Through this Congress the Native Senators in the Union House of Parliament will be able to live in close touch with the Natives of the whole country whose interest each Senator is supposed to represent. The Government also will find a direct and independent channel of informing itself as to the things uppermost in Natives' mind from time to time, and this will make it easier for the Union Government to deal with the Natives of the whole of South Africa. If we wish to convince the Government that it is possible to have a uniform Native policy for the whole of South Africa then let us form this Congress. Again, it is conclusively urgent that this Congress should meet this year, because a matter which is so vitally important to our progress and welfare should not be unnecessarily postponed by reason of personal differences and selfishness of our leaders. The demon of racialism, the aberrations of the Xosa-Fingo feud, the animosity that exists between the Zulus and the Tongas, between the Basutos and every other Native must be buried and forgotten; it has shed among us sufficient blood! We are one people. These divisions, these jealousies, are the cause of all our woes and of all our backwardness and ignorance today.

# 18

## MARCUS GARVEY

## *Speech in Philadelphia*

### *1919*

*Jamaican-born Marcus Garvey (1887–1940) left school at age fourteen to train as a printer. After living for a time in Central America and London, he founded the Universal Negro Improvement Association (UNIA) in Jamaica in 1914. Garvey's hope of gaining Booker T. Washington's support in the United States for this organization was ended by Dr. Washington's death. Nevertheless, Garvey's introduction of the UNIA in Harlem and other cities with large black populations was spectacularly successful; this success was largely due to his fiery oratory. Garvey shared with Dr. Washington a firm belief in black-run enterprises as a means of advancement and also promoted the back-to-Africa movement to the black-ruled states of Liberia and Ethiopia as a means of escaping racial discrimination. Liberia's ruling oligarchy turned down the idea, and only a small number of Garveyites emigrated to Ethiopia. In 1925 Garvey was convicted of mail fraud in connection with his Black Star Line and sent to prison. Two years later he was released and deported to Jamaica. He never recovered his status and died in obscurity in London in 1940.*

We have our foe, our ancient foe, puzzled. He does not know what to do with the New Negro; but the New Negro knows what to do with himself. And the thing that we are going to do is to blast a way to complete independence and to that democracy which they denied us even

Robert A. Hill, ed., *The Marcus Garvey and Universal Negro Improvement Association Papers* (Berkeley: University of California Press, 1983ff), 2:91, 92–93, 94, 96.

after we left the battlefields of France and Flanders. We, the New Negroes, say there is no turning back for us now. There is nothing else but a going forward, and if they squeal in America or anywhere else we are going forward. Why, we are not organized as four hundred millions yet, and they are so scared. Now, what will happen in the next five years when the entire four hundred millions will have been organized? All the lynching in the South will be a thing of the past. We are determined in this association to bring the white man to his senses. We are not going to fight and kill anybody because he has more than we have. But if there is anybody taking advantage of the Negro, whether he be white, red, or blue, we are going to organize to stop him. . . .

I believe in the brotherhood of man. I believe in the fatherhood of God, but as man sinned and lost his purpose ever since the fall of Adam and Eve, I also realize that man has lost his closest connection, his closest tie, with his God. And since man is human, since man has lost his instinct divine, I am not going to trust man. From the attitude of man, from the action of man today, I can see that every one is looking out for himself where the question of race comes in. The white race is looking out for the white race; the yellow race is looking out for the yellow race or Asiatic race. The time has come when the Negro should look out for himself and let the others look out for themselves. This is the new doctrine today. It is the doctrine of Europe. Europe is looking out for the white man. It is the doctrine of Asia. Asia is looking out for the yellow man. So should Africa look out for the black man, the Negro. And since they (the whites) have divided up Africa, having a part in America, a part in Canada, a part in the West Indies, a part in Central America, a part in South America, and a part remaining in Africa, we are saying that the time has come that there should be a united Africa. And before a united Africa comes, Ethiopia, as scattered as she is, must stretch forth her hands unto God. . . .

And I want you men of Africa, you men of the Negro race, to prepare for the day when Africa will call for a judgment. Africa is preparing to call for a judgment, and that judgment we must have, and it will be a judgment in favor of four hundred million oppressed people. And the marshal who will carry out the authority of the court will be the new Toussaint L'Ouverture[1] with the sword and the banner of the new African Republic. You black men of Philadelphia sit here tonight as

---

[1]Toussaint Louverture (ca. 1743–1803), leader of the Haitian Revolution. [Ed.]

jurors in the case where judgment is to be given in favor of the Negro, and I am now asking you jurymen: Gentlemen of the jury, what is your verdict? Cries of: "Africa must be free!" Now, if Africa is to be free, it means, therefore, that Philadelphia has given her verdict as we have in New York. It is now for the judge to give his finding. The judge will give his finding after all the jurors of the Negro race, four hundred million, will have given their verdict. And then after the judge gives his finding he will have to find a marshal to serve the writ, who will require the New Negro to help him to serve this writ, because the man to whom this writ is to be served is of a desperate character, because he prefers to shed blood and take lives before he will give up what is not his. You have to spill blood in Africa before you get what is belonging to you.

## A Negro Government

Therefore, you will realize that the Universal Negro Improvement Association is no joke. It is a serious movement. It is as serious a movement as the movement of the Irish today to have a free Ireland; as the determination of the Jew to recover Palestine. The Negro peoples of the world should be so determined to reclaim Africa and found a government there, so that if any black man in any part of the world is abused we can call the mighty power of Africa to come to our aid. Men, a Negro government we had once, and a Negro government we must have again. Tell me that I must live everlastingly under the domination of a white man, that I must bequeath to my children white overlordship, then I say, let me die now, Almighty God. If there is no better future in the world for me than to be the slave of a white man, I say, take the life you gave me. I do not want it. You would not be my God if you created me to be a slave to other men; but you are my God and will continue to be my God if you created me an equal of all men. . . .

That is why we want the Black Star Line so as to launch out to the Negro peoples of the world, and today the richest people of the world are the Negro people of Africa. Their minerals, their diamonds, their gold and their silver, and their iron have built up the great English, French, German, and Belgian Empires. Men, how long are we going to allow those parasites to suck the blood out of our children? How long? I answer for those who are active members of the Universal Negro Improvement Association and African Communities League, "Not one day longer." No parasite shall continue to feed off my body, because I want to have a healthy body. I have not sufficient blood to give to any parasite, because when I get sick I will need every drop of my blood to sustain me until I am well, so while I am well I will have to take off that parasite and throw it away. The time has come for the Negro to exert his energy to the utmost to do [so]. Men and women of Philadelphia, the question is now for you to decide. Are you ready tonight or are you going to wait for two years more to be ready[?] The answer is, "You must be ready now[.]" Thank God, there are millions of us who are ready already, and when the Black Star Line sails out, by the demonstration of the Black Star Line spontaneously and simultaneously, millions will become [wealthy?].

# 19

## UNIVERSAL NEGRO IMPROVEMENT ASSOCIATION

### Declaration of the Rights of the Negro People of the World

#### 1920

*The following declaration was drafted and adopted at the UNIA convention in New York. At that meeting Marcus Garvey was elected provisional president of Africa.*

Be it Resolved, That the Negro people of the world, through their chosen representatives in convention assembled in Liberty Hall, in the City of New York and United States of America, from August 1 to August 31, in the year of our Lord, one thousand nine hundred and twenty, protest against the wrongs and injustices they are suffering at the hands of their white brethren, and state what they deem their fair and just rights, as well as the treatment they propose to demand of all men in the future.

Raymond Leslie Buell, *The Native Problem in Africa*, vol. II (New York: The Macmillan Co., 1928), 965–69.

We complain:

I. That nowhere in the world, with few exceptions, are black men accorded equal treatment with white men, although in the same situation and circumstances, but, on the contrary, are discriminated against and denied the common rights due to human beings for no other reason than their race and color.

We are not willingly accepted as guests in the public hotels and inns of the world for no other reason than our race and color.

II. In certain parts of the United States of America our race is denied the right of public trial accorded to other races when accused of crime, but are lynched and burned by mobs, and such brutal and inhuman treatment is even practiced upon our women.

III. That European nations have parcelled out among themselves and taken possession of nearly all of the continent of Africa, and the natives are compelled to surrender their lands to aliens and are treated in most instances like slaves.

IV. In the southern portion of the United States of America, although citizens under the Federal Constitution, and in some states, almost equal to the whites in population and are qualified land owners and taxpayers, we are, nevertheless, denied all voice in the making and administration of the laws and are taxed without representation by the state governments, and at the same time compelled to do military service in defense of the country.

V. On the public conveyances and common carriers in the Southern portion of the United States we are jim-crowed and compelled to accept separate and inferior accommodations and made to pay the same fare charged for first-class accommodations, and our families are often humiliated and insulted by drunken white men who habitually pass through the jim-crow cars going to the smoking car.

VI. The physicians of our race are denied the right to attend their patients while in the public hospitals of the cities and states where they reside in certain parts of the United States.

Our children are forced to attend inferior separate schools for shorter terms than white children, and the public school funds are unequally divided between the white and colored schools.

VII. We are discriminated against and denied an equal chance to earn wages for the support of our families, and in many instances are refused admission into labor unions, and nearly everywhere are paid smaller wages than white men.

VIII. In Civil Service and departmental offices we are everywhere discriminated against and made to feel that to be a black man in Europe, America, and the West Indies is equivalent to being an outcast and a leper among the races of men, no matter what the character and attainments of the black man may be.

IX. In the British and other West Indian Islands and colonies, Negroes are secretly and cunningly discriminated against, and denied those fuller rights in government to which white citizens are appointed, nominated, and elected.

X. That our people in those parts are forced to work for lower wages than the average standard of white men and are kept in conditions repugnant to good civilized tastes and customs.

XI. That the many acts of injustice against members of our race before the courts of law in the respective islands and colonies are of such nature as to create disgust and disrespect for the white man's sense of justice.

XII. Against all such inhuman, unchristian, and uncivilized treatment we here and now emphatically protest, and invoke the condemnation of all mankind.

In order to encourage our race all over the world and to stimulate it to a higher and grander destiny, we demand and insist on the following Declaration of Rights:

1. Be it known to all men that whereas, all men are created equal and entitled to the rights of life, liberty, and the pursuit of happiness, and because of this we, the duly elected representatives of the Negro peoples of the world, invoking the aid of the just and Almighty God do declare all men, women, and children of our blood throughout the world free citizens, and do claim them as free citizens of Africa, the Motherland of all Negroes.

2. That we believe in the supreme authority of our race in all things racial; that all things are created and given to man as a common possession; that there should be an equitable distribution and apportionment of all such things, and in consideration of the fact that as a race we are now deprived of those things that are morally and legally ours, we believe it right that all such things should be acquired and held by whatsoever means possible.

3. That we believe the Negro, like any other race, should be governed by the ethics of civilization, and therefore, should not be

deprived of any of those rights or privileges common to other human beings.

4. We declare that Negroes wheresoever they form a community among themselves, should be given the right to elect their own representatives to represent them in legislatures, courts of law, or such institutions as may exercise control over that particular community.

5. We assert that the Negro is entitled to even-handed justice before all courts of law and equity in whatever country he may be found, and when this is denied him on account of his race or color such denial is an insult to the race as a whole and should be resented by the entire body of Negroes.

6. We declare it unfair and prejudicial to the rights of Negroes in communities where they exist in considerable numbers to be tried by a judge and jury composed entirely of an alien race, but in all such cases members of our race are entitled to representation on the jury.

7. We believe that any law or practice that tends to deprive any African of his land or the privileges of free citizenship within his country is unjust and immoral, and no native should respect any such law or practice.

8. We declare taxation without representation unjust and tyrannous, and there should be no obligation on the part of the Negro to obey the levy of a tax by any law-making body from which he is excluded and denied representation on account of his race and color.

9. We believe that any law especially directed against the Negro to his detriment and singling him out because of his race or color is unfair and immoral, and should not be respected.

10. We believe all men entitled to common human respect, and that our race should in no way tolerate any insults that may be interpreted to mean disrespect to our color.

11. We deprecate the use of the term "nigger" as applied to Negroes, and demand that the word "Negro" be written with a capital "N."

12. We believe that the Negro should adopt every means to protect himself against barbarous practices inflicted upon him because of color.

13. We believe in the freedom of Africa for the Negro people of the world, and by the principle of Europe for the Europeans and Asia for the Asiatics; we also demand Africa for the Africans at home and abroad.

14. We believe in the inherent right of the Negro to possess himself of Africa, and that his possession of same shall not be regarded as an infringement on any claim or purchase made by any race or nation.

15. We strongly condemn the cupidity of those nations of the world who, by open aggression or secret schemes, have seized the territories and inexhaustible natural wealth of Africa, and we place on record our most solemn determination to reclaim the treasures and possession of the vast continent of our forefathers.

16. We believe all men should live in peace one with the other, but when races and nations provoke the ire of other races and nations by attempting to infringe upon their rights, war becomes inevitable, and the attempt in any way to free one's self or protect one's rights or heritage becomes justifiable.

17. Whereas, the lynching, by burning, hanging, or any other disgrace to civilization, we therefore declare any country guilty of such atrocities outside the pale of civilization.

18. We protest against the atrocious crime of whipping, flogging, and overworking of the native tribes of Africa and Negroes everywhere. These are methods that should be abolished, and all means should be taken to prevent a continuance of such brutal practices.

19. We protest against the atrocious practice of shaving the heads of Africans, especially of African women or individuals of Negro blood, when placed in prison as a punishment for crime by an alien race.

20. We protest against segregated districts, separate public conveyances, industrial discrimination, lynchings, and limitations of political privileges of any Negro citizen in any part of the world on account of race, color, or creed, and will exert our full influence and power against all such.

21. We protest against any punishment inflicted upon a Negro with severity, as against lighter punishment inflicted upon another of an alien race for like offense, as an act of prejudice and injustice, and should be resented by the entire race.

22. We protest against the system of education in any country where Negroes are denied the same privileges and advantages as other races.

23. We declare it inhuman and unfair to boycott Negroes from industries and labor in any part of the world.

24. We believe in the doctrine of the freedom of the press, and we therefore emphatically protest against the suppression of Negro newspapers and periodicals in various parts of the world, and call upon Negroes everywhere to employ all available means to prevent such suppression.

25. We further demand free speech universally for all men.

26. We hereby protest against the publication of scandalous and inflammatory articles by an alien press tending to create racial strife and the exhibition of picture films showing the Negro as a cannibal.

27. We believe in the self-determination of all peoples.

28. We declare for the freedom of religious worship.

29. With the help of Almighty God, we declare ourselves the sworn protectors of the honor and virtue of our women and children, and pledge our lives for their protection and defense everywhere, and under all circumstances from wrongs and outrages.

30. We demand the right of unlimited and unprejudiced education for ourselves and our posterity forever.

31. We declare that the teaching in any school by alien teachers to our boys and girls, that the alien race is superior to the Negro race, is an insult to the Negro people of the world.

32. Where Negroes form a part of the citizenry of any country, and pass the civil service examination of such country, we declare them entitled to the same consideration as other citizens as to appointments in such civil service.

33. We vigorously protest against the increasingly unfair and unjust treatment accorded Negro travelers on land and sea by the agents and employees of railroad and steamship companies and insist that for equal fare we receive equal privileges with travelers of other races.

34. We declare it unjust for any country, State, or nation to enact laws tending to hinder and obstruct the free immigration of Negroes on account of their race and color.

35. That the right of the Negro to travel unmolested throughout the world be not abridged by any person or persons, and all Negroes are called upon to give aid to a fellow Negro when thus molested.

36. We declare that all Negroes are entitled to the same right to travel over the world as other men.

37. We hereby demand that the governments of the world recognize our leader and his representatives chosen by the race to look after the welfare of our people under such governments.

38. We demand complete control of our social institutions without interference by any alien race or races.

39. That the colors, Red, Black and Green, be the colors of the Negro race.

# 20

## C. L. R. JAMES

# The West Indian Contribution to Pan-Africanism

### 1921–1959

*Born in Trinidad, C. L. R. James (1901–1989) worked in his home country as a teacher before moving to Great Britain, where he worked as a sports reporter and was active in Pan-Africanist circles. From 1938 to 1953 he lived in the United States until he was expelled for his socialist views. He was allowed to return in 1970 and taught at Federal City College. Among his many books are* Beyond a Boundary *(1963) (on cricket and colonialism), plays, novels, political analyses, histories, and criticism. He is best known for* The Black Jacobins: Toussaint L'Ouverture and the San Domingo Revolution *(1938), from whose appendix to the 1963 edition the following analysis of early Pan-Africanism is taken.*

The story is one of the strangest stories in any period of history. The individual facts are known. But no one has ever put them together and drawn to them the attention they deserve. Today the emancipation of Africa is one of the outstanding events of contemporary history. Between the wars when this emancipation was being prepared, the unquestioned leaders of the movement in every public sphere, in Africa itself, in Europe, and in the United States, were not Africans but West Indians. First the unquestioned facts.

Two black West Indians using the ink of Negritude wrote their names imperishably on the front pages of the history of our time. Standing at the head is Marcus Garvey. Garvey, an immigrant from Jamaica, is the only Negro who has succeeded in building a mass movement among American Negroes. Arguments about the number of his followers dispute the number of millions. Garvey advocated the return of Africa to the Africans and people of African descent. He

---

"From Toussaint L'Ouverture to Fidel Castro," appendix to *The Black Jacobins: Toussaint L'Ouverture and the San Domingo Revolution*, 2nd ed. (New York: Vintage Books, 1963), 396–99.

organized, very rashly and incompetently, the Black Star Line, a steamship company for transporting people of African descent from the New World back to Africa. Garvey did not last long. His movement took really effective form in about 1921, and by 1926 he was in a United States prison (some charge about misusing the mails); from prison he was deported home to Jamaica. But all this is only the frame and scaffolding. Garvey never set foot in Africa. He spoke no African language. His conceptions of Africa seemed to be a West Indian island and West Indian people multiplied a thousand times over. But Garvey managed to convey to Negroes everywhere (and to the rest of the world) his passionate belief that Africa was the home of a civilization which had once been great and would be great again. When you bear in mind the slenderness of his resources, the vast material forces and the pervading social conceptions which automatically sought to destroy him, his achievement remains one of the propagandistic miracles of this century.

Garvey's voice reverberated inside Africa itself. The King of Swaziland told Mrs. Marcus Garvey that he knew the name of only two black men in the Western world: Jack Johnson, the boxer who defeated the white man Jim Jeffries, and Marcus Garvey. Jomo Kenyatta has related to this writer how in 1921 Kenya nationalists, unable to read, would gather round a reader of Garvey's newspaper, the *Negro World*, and listen to an article two or three times. Then they would run various ways through the forest, carefully to repeat the whole, which they had memorized, to Africans hungry for some doctrine which lifted them from the servile consciousness in which Africans lived. Dr. Nkrumah, a graduate student of history and philosophy at two American universities, has placed it on record that of all the writers who educated and influenced him, Marcus Garvey stands first. Garvey found the cause of Africans and of people of African descent not so much neglected as unworthy of consideration. In little more than half of ten years he had made it a part of the political consciousness of the world. He did not know the word Negritude but he knew the thing. With enthusiasm he would have welcomed the nomenclature, with justice claimed paternity.

The other British West Indian was from Trinidad, George Padmore. Padmore shook the dust of the cramping West Indies from his feet in the early 1920's and went to the United States. When he died in 1959, eight countries sent representatives to his funeral, which was held in London. His ashes were interred in Ghana; and all assert that in that country of political demonstrations, there never has been a political demonstration such as was evoked by these obsequies of Padmore. Peasants from remote areas who, it could have been thought, had never heard his name, found their way to Accra to pay the last tribute to this West Indian who had spent his life in their service.

Once in America he became an active Communist. He was moved to Moscow to head their Negro department of propaganda and organization. In that post he became the best known and most trusted of agitators for African independence. In 1935, seeking alliances, the Kremlin separated Britain and France as "democratic imperialisms" from Germany and Japan, making the "Fascist imperialisms" the main target of Russian and Communist propaganda. This reduced activity for African emancipation to a farce: Germany and Japan had no colonies in Africa. Padmore broke instantly with the Kremlin. He went to London where, in a single room, he earned a meagre living by journalism, to be able to continue the work he had done in the Kremlin. He wrote books and pamphlets, attended all anti-imperialist meetings, and spoke and moved resolutions wherever possible. He made and maintained an ever-increasing range of nationalist contacts in all sections of African society and the colonial world. He preached and taught Pan-Africanism and organized an African Bureau. He published a journal devoted to African emancipation (the present writer was its editor).

This is no place to attempt even a summary of the work and influence of the most striking West Indian creation between the wars, Padmore's African Bureau. Between the wars it was the only African organization of its kind in existence. Of the seven members of the committee, five were West Indians, and they ran the organization. Of them, only Padmore had ever visited Africa. It could not have been accidental that this West Indian attracted two of the most remarkable Africans of this or any other time. A founder-member and a simmering volcano of African nationalism was Jomo Kenyatta. But even better fortune was in store for us.

The present writer met Nkrumah, then a student at the University of Pennsylvania, and wrote to Padmore about him. Nkrumah came to England to study law and there formed an association with Padmore; they worked at the doctrines and premises of Pan-Africanism and elaborated the plans which culminated in Nkrumah's leading the people of the Gold Coast to the independence of Ghana. This revolution by the Gold Coast was the blow which made so many cracks in the piece of African colonialism that it proved impossible ever to stick them together again. With Nkrumah's victory the association did not cease.

After independence was signed and sealed, Nkrumah sent for Padmore, installed him once more in an office devoted to African emancipation and, under the auspices of an African government, this West Indian, as he had done in 1931 under the auspices of the Kremlin, organized in Accra the first conference of independent African states, followed, twenty-five years after the first, by the second world conference of fighters for African freedom. Dr. Banda, Patrice Lumumba, Nyerere, Tom Mboya, were some of those who attended the conference. Jomo Kenyatta was not there only because he was in jail. NBC made a national telecast of the interment of his ashes in Christiansborg Castle, at which Padmore was designated the Father of African Emancipation, a distinction challenged by no one.

## 21

### KWAME NKRUMAH

*Pan-Africanism and African Nationalism*

*1937–1958*

*The son of a goldsmith, Kwame Nkrumah (ca. 1909–1972) attended Catholic mission schools and a teacher training college in the British colony of the Gold Coast. In his youth he dreamed of becoming a priest, but his destiny would be in politics. Following in the footsteps of other West Africans, he chose to study in the United States from 1935, earning degrees from Lincoln University and the University of Pennsylvania and teaching for a time at Lincoln. Like other African students, he had to work to pay his tuition and other expenses, finally abandoning plans to earn a doctorate when he could no longer stand the strain of working nights on the docks of Philadelphia. In 1945 Nkrumah went to Great Britain, where, as he relates in this selection, he, along with the Trinidadian George Padmore, co-organized the Fifth Pan-African Congress. Nkrumah was active in African nationalist groups before returning to the Gold Coast in 1947 as a political organizer. He soon formed his own*

Kwame Nkrumah, *Africa Must Unite* (New York: International Publishers, 1963), 134–36.

*political party, the Convention People's Party, and his fiery populist oratory enabled him to win the colony's first national elections in 1951, even while jailed for suspected sedition. Released from prison, he took charge of the colony's government, and at independence in 1957 Nkrumah became the first president of the renamed Republic of Ghana. These achievements made him the hero of African nationalists and blacks around the Atlantic. Nkrumah was also a fervent supporter of Pan-Africanism. His increasingly erratic rule ended when Ghana's army deposed him in 1966.*

A non-party organization, the International African Service Bureau, was set up in 1937, and this was the forerunner of the Pan-African federation, the British section of the Pan-African Congress movement. Its aim was "to promote the well-being and unity of African peoples and peoples of African descent throughout the world," and also "to strive to co-operate between African peoples and others who share our aspirations."

Pan-Africanism and African nationalism really took concrete expression when the Fifth Pan-African Congress met in Manchester in 1945. For the first time the necessity for well-organized, firmly-knit movements as a primary condition for the success of the national liberation struggle in Africa was stressed.

The Congress was attended by more than two hundred delegates from all over the world. George Padmore and I had been joint secretaries of the organizational committee which planned the Congress and we were delighted with the results of our work. Among the declarations addressed to the imperialist powers asserting the determination of the colonial people to be free was the following:

> The Fifth Pan-African Congress calls on intellectuals and professional classes of the Colonies to awaken to their responsibilities. The long, long night is over. By fighting for trade union rights, the right to form co-operatives, freedom of the press, assembly, demonstration, and strike, freedom to print and read the literature which is necessary for the education of the masses, you will be using the only means by which your liberties will be won and maintained. Today there is only one road to effective action—the organization of the masses.*

*Declaration to the Colonial Peoples of the World (by the present author [Nkrumah]), approved and adopted by the Pan-African Congress held in Manchester, England, 15–21 October 1945.

W. E. B. Du Bois and Kwame Nkrumah at the Presidential Palace, Ghana, 1963.
Reproduced with permission of the Special Collections Department, W. E. B. Du Bois
Library, University of Massachusetts Amherst.

A definite programme of action was agreed upon. Basically, the programme centered round the demand for constitutional change, providing for universal suffrage. The methods to be employed were based
on the Gandhist technique of non-violent non-co-operation, in other
words, the withholding of labor, civil disobedience, and economic
boycott. There were to be variations of emphasis from territory to territory according to the differing circumstances. The fundamental purpose was identical: national independence leading to African unity.
The limited objective was combined with the wider perspective.

Instead of a rather nebulous movement, concerned vaguely with
black nationalism, the Pan-African movement had become an expression of African nationalism. Unlike the first four Congresses, which had

been supported mainly by middle-class intellectuals and bourgeois reformists, the Fifth Pan-African Congress was attended by workers, trade unionists, farmers, and students, most of whom came from Africa.

When the Congress ended, having agreed on the programme for Pan-African nationalism, a working committee was set up with DuBois as chairman and myself as general secretary. The Congress headquarters were moved to London, where shortly afterwards the West African National Secretariat was also established. Its purpose was to put into action, in West Africa, the policies agreed upon in Manchester. I was offered, and accepted, the secretaryship.

We published a monthly paper called *The New African*, and called two West African Conferences in London. By this time the political conscience of African students was thoroughly aroused, and they talked of little else but the colonial liberation movement. The more enthusiastic among us formed a kind of inner group which we called *The Circle*. Only those working genuinely for West African freedom and unity were admitted, and we began to prepare ourselves actively for revolutionary work in any part of the African continent.

It was at this point that I was asked to return to the Gold Coast to become general secretary of the United Gold Coast Convention. I accepted with some hesitation. There was my work for the West African National Secretariat to consider, and also the preparations which were being made for the calling of a West African National Conference in Lagos in October 1948.

I called at Freetown and Monrovia on the way home, and spoke with African nationalists there, telling them of the conference plans and urging them to attend. The political contacts I made in both Sierra Leone and Liberia were to prove significant later, though the conference in Lagos never, in fact, took place.

When I returned to West Africa in 1947, it was with the intention of using the Gold Coast as a starting-off point for African independence and unity. With the mass movement I was able to build up in the Convention People's Party, the Gold Coast secured its freedom and emerged as the sovereign state of Ghana in 1957. I at once made it clear that there would be no meaning to the national independence of Ghana unless it was linked with the total liberation of the African continent. While our independence celebrations were actually taking place, I called for a conference of all the sovereign states of Africa, to discuss plans for the future of our continent.

The first Conference of Independent African States met in Accra in April 1958. There were then only eight, namely, Egypt, Ghana,

Sudan, Libya, Tunisia, Liberia, Morocco, and Ethiopia. Our purpose was to exchange views on matters of common interest; to explore ways and means of consolidating and safeguarding our independence; to strengthen the economic and cultural ties between our countries; to decide on workable arrangements for helping fellow Africans still subject to colonial rule; and to examine the central world problem of how to secure peace.

When, on 15 April 1958, I welcomed the representatives to the conference, I felt that at last Pan-Africanism had moved to the African continent where it really belonged. It was an historic occasion. Free Africans were actually meeting together, *in Africa*, to examine and consider African affairs. Here was a signal departure from established custom, a jar to the arrogant assumption of non-African nations that African affairs were solely the concern of states outside our continent. The African personality was making itself known.

Because many of the speeches made at the conference were similar in content, it was alleged in some quarters that there had been previous collaboration. I am able to state categorically that all of us who spoke had prepared our speeches independently. If they showed identity of thought and belief, it was because our attitudes in Africa were assuming an identity of vision and purpose.

# 4
# Black Cultural Unity and Global Agendas, 1904–1966

## 22

### HAILE SELASSIE I

## An Appeal to the League of Nations

### 1936

*Originally named Tafari Makonnen (1892–1975), this member of the royal family of the kingdom of Shoa assumed the name Haile Selassie when he was crowned* negus nagast *("king of kings" or "emperor") of Ethiopia in 1930. He had already been acting as head of the country's government since 1916, when he became regent for the previous emperor's daughter. As regent he used the honorific title* Ras *(roughly meaning "duke"). Ras Tafari had succeeded in gaining membership for Ethiopia in the League of Nations, the only black-ruled state other than Liberia to be a member. His efforts at reforming the mountainous state were interrupted when Italy invaded in 1935. While he was in Europe delivering this appeal to the League of Nations, the Italians completed their conquest. During World War II the British drove out the Italians and restored Haile Selassie to his throne in 1941. He continued his program of gradual reform, creating a secular educational system and an elected legislature. In the 1960s he was very active promoting inter-African unity, offering his capital, Addis Ababa, as the headquarters of the Organization of African Unity. After nearly six decades in power, he was overthrown by a coup in 1974. A Jamaican-founded sect, the Rastafarians, revere Haile Selassie as a deity.*

From Haile Selassie's speech to the League of Nations, 30 June 1936. Courtesy of nazret.com.

Emperor Haile Selassie addressing the League of Nations, 1936.
Reproduced with the permission of Keystone Press Agency.

I, Haile Selassie I, Emperor of Ethiopia, am here today to claim that justice which is due to my people, and the assistance promised to it eight months ago, when fifty nations asserted that aggression had been committed in violation of international treaties.

There is no precedent for a Head of State himself speaking in this assembly. But there is also no precedent for a people being victim of such injustice and being at present threatened by abandonment to its aggressor. Also, there has never before been an example of any Government proceeding to the systematic extermination of a nation by barbarous means, in violation of the most solemn promises made by the nations of the earth that there should not be used against innocent human beings the terrible poison of harmful gases. It is to defend a people struggling for its age-old independence that the head of the Ethiopian Empire has come to Geneva to fulfil this supreme duty, after having himself fought at the head of his armies.

I pray to Almighty God that He may spare nations the terrible suf-ferings that have just been inflicted on my people, and of which the chiefs who accompany me here have been the horrified witnesses.

It is my duty to inform the Governments assembled in Geneva, responsible as they are for the lives of millions of men, women, and children, of the deadly peril which threatens them, by describing to them the fate which has been suffered by Ethiopia. It is not only upon warriors that the Italian Government has made war. It has above all attacked populations far removed from hostilities, in order to terrorize and exterminate them.

At the beginning, towards the end of 1935, Italian aircraft hurled upon my armies bombs of tear-gas. Their effects were but slight. The soldiers learned to scatter, waiting until the wind had rapidly dis-persed the poisonous gases. The Italian aircraft then resorted to mus-tard gas. Barrels of liquid were hurled upon armed groups. But this means also was not effective; the liquid affected only a few soldiers, and barrels upon the ground were themselves a warning to troops and to the population of the danger.

It was at the time when the operations for the encircling of Ma-kalle[1] were taking place that the Italian command, fearing a rout, fol-lowed the procedure which it is now my duty to denounce to the world. Special sprayers were installed on board aircraft so that they could vaporize, over vast areas of territory, a fine, death-dealing rain. Groups of nine, fifteen, eighteen aircraft followed one another so that the fog issuing from them formed a continuous sheet. It was thus that, as from the end of January, 1936, soldiers, women, children, cattle, rivers, lakes, and pastures were drenched continually with this deadly rain. In order to kill off systematically all living creatures, in order to more surely poison waters and pastures, the Italian command made its aircraft pass over and over again. That was its chief method of warfare.

### Ravage and Terror

The very refinement of barbarism consisted in carrying ravage and terror into the most densely populated parts of the territory, the points farthest removed from the scene of hostilities. The object was

---

[1] Mekele, town in northern Ethiopia. [Ed.]

to scatter fear and death over a great part of the Ethiopian territory. These fearful tactics succeeded. Men and animals succumbed. The deadly rain that fell from the aircraft made all those whom it touched fly shrieking with pain. All those who drank the poisoned water or ate the infected food also succumbed in dreadful suffering. In tens of thousands, the victims of the Italian mustard gas fell. It is in order to denounce to the civilized world the tortures inflicted upon the Ethiopian people that I resolved to come to Geneva. None other than myself and my brave companions in arms could bring the League of Nations the undeniable proof. The appeals of my delegates addressed to the League of Nations had remained without any answer; my delegates had not been witnesses. That is why I decided to come myself to bear witness against the crime perpetrated against my people and give Europe a warning of the doom that awaits it, if it should bow before the accomplished fact.

Is it necessary to remind the Assembly of the various stages of the Ethiopian drama? For 20 years past, either as Heir Apparent, Regent of the Empire, or as Emperor, I have never ceased to use all my efforts to bring my country the benefits of civilization, and in particular to establish relations of good neighborliness with adjacent powers. In particular I succeeded in concluding with Italy the Treaty of Friendship of 1928, which absolutely prohibited the resort, under any pretext whatsoever, to force of arms, substituting for force and pressure the conciliation and arbitration on which civilized nations have based international order. . . .

## Covenant Violated

Those are the terms of the report of the Committee of Thirteen. The Council and the Assembly unanimously adopted the conclusion that the Italian Government had violated the Covenant and was in a state of aggression. I did not hesitate to declare that I did not wish for war, that it was imposed upon me, and I should struggle solely for the independence and integrity of my people, and that in that struggle I was the defender of the cause of all small States exposed to the greed of a powerful neighbor.

In October, 1935, the fifty-two nations who are listening to me today gave me an assurance that the aggressor would not triumph, that the resources of the Covenant would be employed in order to ensure the reign of right and the failure of violence.

I ask the fifty-two nations not to forget today the policy upon which they embarked eight months ago, and on faith of which I directed the resistance of my people against the aggressor whom they had denounced to the world. Despite the inferiority of my weapons, the complete lack of aircraft, artillery, munitions, hospital services, my confidence in the League was absolute. I thought it to be impossible that fifty-two nations, including the most powerful in the world, should be successfully opposed by a single aggressor. Counting on the faith due to treaties, I had made no preparation for war, and that is the case with certain small countries in Europe.

When the danger became more urgent, being aware of my responsibilities towards my people, during the first six months of 1935 I tried to acquire armaments. Many Governments proclaimed an embargo to prevent my doing so, whereas the Italian Government through the Suez Canal, was given all facilities for transporting without cessation and without protest, troops, arms, and munitions.

### Forced to Mobilize

On October 3rd, 1935, the Italian troops invaded my territory. A few hours later only I decreed general mobilization. In my desire to maintain peace I had, following the example of a great country in Europe on the eve of the Great War, caused my troops to withdraw thirty kilometers so as to remove any pretext of provocation.

War then took place in the atrocious conditions which I have laid before the Assembly. In that unequal struggle between a Government commanding more than forty-two million inhabitants, having at its disposal financial, industrial, and technical means which enabled it to create unlimited quantities of the most death-dealing weapons, and, on the other hand, a small people of twelve million inhabitants, without arms, without resources[,] having on its side only the justice of its own cause and the promise of the League of Nations. What real assistance was given to Ethiopia by the fifty-two nations who had declared the Rome Government guilty of a breach of the Covenant and had undertaken to prevent the triumph of the aggressor? Has each of the States Members, as it was its duty to do in virtue of its signature appended to Article 15 of the Covenant, considered the aggressor as having committed an act of war personally directed against itself? I had placed all my hopes in the execution of these undertakings. My confidence had been confirmed by the repeated declarations made in the Council to the effect that aggression must not be rewarded, and that force would end by being compelled to bow before right. . . .

## League Threatened

It is collective security: it is the very existence of the League of Nations. It is the confidence that each State is to place in international treaties. It is the value of promises made to small States that their integrity and their independence shall be respected and ensured. It is the principle of the equality of States on the one hand, or otherwise the obligation laid upon small Powers to accept the bonds of vassalship. In a word, it is international morality that is at stake. Have the signatures appended to a Treaty value only in so far as the signatory Powers have a personal, direct, and immediate interest involved?

No subtlety can change the problem or shift the grounds of the discussion. It is in all sincerity that I submit these considerations to the Assembly. At a time when my people are threatened with extermination, when the support of the League may ward off the final blow, may I be allowed to speak with complete frankness, without reticence, in all directness such as is demanded by the rule of equality as between all States Members of the League?

Apart from the Kingdom of the Lord there is not on this earth any nation that is superior to any other. Should it happen that a strong Government finds it may with impunity destroy a weak people, then the hour strikes for that weak people to appeal to the League of Nations to give its judgment in all freedom. God and history will remember your judgment.

## Assistance Refused

I have heard it asserted that the inadequate sanctions already applied have not achieved their object. At no time, and under no circumstances could sanctions that were intentionally inadequate, intentionally badly applied, stop an aggressor. This is not a case of the impossibility of stopping an aggressor but of the refusal to stop an aggressor. When Ethiopia requested and requests that she should be given financial assistance, was that a measure which it was impossible to apply whereas financial assistance of the League has been granted, even in times of peace, to two countries and exactly to two countries who have refused to apply sanctions against the aggressor?

Faced by numerous violations by the Italian Government of all international treaties that prohibit resort to arms, and the use of barbarous methods of warfare, it is my painful duty to note that the initiative has today been taken with a view to raising sanctions. Does this initiative not mean in practice the abandonment of Ethiopia to the aggressor? On the very eve of the day when I was about to attempt a supreme effort in the defense of my people before this Assembly does not this initiative deprive Ethiopia of one of her last chances to succeed in obtaining the support and guarantee of States Members? Is that the guidance the League of Nations and each of the States Members are entitled to expect from the great Powers when they assert their right and their duty to guide the action of the League? Placed by the aggressor face to face with the accomplished fact, are States going to set up the terrible precedent of bowing before force?

Your Assembly will doubtless have laid before it proposals for the reform of the Covenant and for rendering more effective the guarantee of collective security. Is it the Covenant that needs reform? What undertakings can have any value if the will to keep them is lacking? It is international morality which is at stake and not the Articles of the Covenant. On behalf of the Ethiopian people, a member of the League of Nations, I request the Assembly to take all measures proper to ensure respect for the Covenant. I renew my protest against the violations of treaties of which the Ethiopian people has been the victim. I declare in the face of the whole world that the Emperor, the Government, and the people of Ethiopia will not bow before force; that they maintain their claims that they will use all means in their power to ensure the triumph of right and the respect of the Covenant.

I ask the fifty-two nations, who have given the Ethiopian people a promise to help them in their resistance to the aggressor, what are they willing to do for Ethiopia? And the great Powers who have promised the guarantee of collective security to small States on whom weighs the threat that they may one day suffer the fate of Ethiopia, I ask what measures do you intend to take?

Representatives of the World[,] I have come to Geneva to discharge in your midst the most painful of the duties of the head of a State. What reply shall I have to take back to my people?

# 23

## RALPH J. BUNCHE

# Peace and a Better Life for All Men

### 1950

---

*After his parents died when he was twelve, Ralph J. Bunche (1904–1971) was raised in Los Angeles by his grandmother, who had been born in slavery. An outstanding student and athlete, he won an athletic scholarship to the University of California at Los Angeles, where he played basketball, and graduated in international relations at the top of his class. UCLA later named a large building after him. He won fellowships to study political science at Harvard University and earned a master's degree in 1928. While completing his Ph.D. dissertation on French rule in Africa, and after receiving his Ph.D. in 1934, Bunche taught at Howard University and did postdoctoral research at Northwestern University, the London School of Economics, and the University of Cape Town. He taught at Harvard University from 1950 to 1952. Active in civil rights struggles, his tone was always moderate and reasonable but nonetheless effective, as when he declined President Truman's appointment as an assistant secretary of state in protest against the racial segregation prevalent in Washington, D.C. During World War II he had worked for the Office of Strategic Services (forerunner of the Central Intelligence Agency), and in 1946 he was "borrowed" from his State Department position to head up the new United Nations' Department of Trusteeship, overseeing territories moving from colonial rule to independence under UN supervision. The peak of his career was his involvement in bringing about a peaceful settlement to the Israeli-Palestinian conflicts of 1947–1949, for which he was given many honors, including the Nobel Peace Prize for 1950. This selection is from his Nobel Prize address.*

---

In this most anxious period of human history, the subject of peace, above every other, commands the solemn attention of all men of

---

Ralph J. Bunche, "Some Reflections on Peace in Our Time," Nobel Lecture, 11 Dec. 1950, © The Nobel Foundation, 1950.

reason and goodwill. Moreover, on this particular occasion, marking the fiftieth anniversary of the Nobel Foundation, it is eminently fitting to speak of peace. No subject could be closer to my own heart, since I have the honor to speak as a member of the international Secretariat of the United Nations.

In these critical times—times which test to the utmost the good sense, the forbearance, and the morality of every peace-loving people—it is not easy to speak of peace with either conviction or reassurance. True it is that statesmen the world over, exalting lofty concepts and noble ideals, pay homage to peace and freedom in a perpetual torrent of eloquent phrases. But the statesmen also speak darkly of the lurking threat of war; and the preparations for war ever intensify, while strife flares or threatens in many localities. . . .

In its short but turbulent five years, the United Nations, until the past few weeks, at least, has demonstrated a comforting ability to cope with every dangerous crisis that has erupted into violence or threatened to do so. It has never been easily done nor as well as might be hoped for, but the fact remains that it has been done. In these post-war years, the United Nations, in the interest of peace, has been called upon to eliminate the threat of local wars, to stop local wars already underway, and now in Korea, itself to undertake an international police action which amounts to full-scale war. Its record has been impressive. Its interventions have been directly responsible for checking and containing dangerous armed conflicts in Indonesia, Kashmir, and Palestine, and to only a lesser extent in Greece. . . .

To make peace in the world secure, the United Nations must have readily at its disposal, as a result of firm commitments undertaken by all of its members, military strength of sufficient dimensions to make it certain that it can meet aggressive military force with international military force, speedily and conclusively.

If that kind of strength is made available to the United Nations— and under action taken by the General Assembly this fall it can be made available—in my view that strength will never again be challenged in war and therefore need never be employed.

But military strength will not be enough. The moral position of the United Nations must ever be strong and unassailable; it must stand steadfastly, always, for the right.

The international problems with which the United Nations is concerned are the problems of the interrelations of the peoples of the world. They are human problems. The United Nations is entitled to believe, and it does believe, that there are no insoluble problems of human relations and that there is none which cannot be solved by peaceful means. The United Nations—in Indonesia, Palestine, and Kashmir—has demonstrated convincingly that parties to the most severe conflict may be induced to abandon war as the method of settlement in favor of mediation and conciliation, at a merciful saving of untold lives and acute suffering.

Unfortunately, there may yet be some in the world who have not learned that today war can settle nothing, that aggressive force can never be enough, nor will it be tolerated. If this should be so, the pitiless wrath of the organized world must fall upon those who would endanger the peace for selfish ends. For in this advanced day, there is no excuse, no justification, for nations resorting to force except to repel armed attack.

The world and its peoples being as they are, there is no easy or quick or infallible approach to a secure peace. It is only by patient, persistent, undismayed effort, by trial and error, that peace can be won. Nor can it be won cheaply, as the taxpayer is learning. In the existing world tension, there will be rebuffs and setbacks, dangerous crises, and episodes of violence. But the United Nations, with unshakable resolution, in the future as in the past, will continue to man the dikes of peace. In this common purpose, all states, irrespective of size, are vital.

The small nations, which constitute the overwhelming majority in its membership, are a great source of strength for the United Nations. Their desire for peace is deep seated and constant. The fear, suspicion, and conflict which characterize the relations among the great powers, and the resultant uncertainty, keep them and their peoples in a state of anxious tension and suspense. For the relations among the great powers will largely determine their future. A third world war would quickly engulf the smaller states, and many of them would again provide the battlefields. On many of them, now as before, the impact of war would be even more severe than upon the great powers. They in particular, therefore, support and often initiate measures designed to ensure that the United Nations shall be increasingly effective as a practical instrumentality for peace. In this regard, the Scandinavian countries contribute signally to the constructive effort of the United Nations.

. . . Europe, and the Western world generally, must become fully aware that the massive and restive millions of Asia and Africa are henceforth a new and highly significant factor in all peace calculations. These hitherto suppressed masses are rapidly awakening and are demanding, and are entitled to enjoy, a full share in the future fruits of peace, freedom, and security.

Very many of these millions are experiencing a newfound freedom. Many other millions are still in subject status as colonials. The aspirations and demands of those who have achieved freedom and those who seek it are the same: security, treatment as equals, and their rightful place in the brotherhood of nations.

It is truer today than when Alfred Nobel realized it a half-century ago, that peace cannot be achieved in a vacuum. Peace must be paced by human progress. Peace is no mere matter of men fighting or not fighting. Peace, to have meaning for many who have known only suffering in both peace and war, must be translated into bread or rice, shelter, health, and education, as well as freedom and human dignity—a steadily better life. If peace is to be secure, long-suffering and long-starved, forgotten peoples of the world, the underprivileged and the undernourished, must begin to realize without delay the promise of a new day and a new life.

In the world of today, Europe, like the rest of the West, is confronted with the urgent necessity of a new orientation—a global orientation. The pre-war outlook is as obsolete as the pre-war world. There must be an awakening to the incontestable fact that the far away, little known, and little understood peoples of Asia and Africa, who constitute the majority of the world's population, are no longer passive and no longer to be ignored. The fury of the world ideological struggle swirls about them. Their vast numbers will prove a dominant factor in the future world pattern of life. They provide virgin soil for the growth of democracy, but the West must first learn how to approach them understandingly and how to win their trust and friendship. There is a long and unsavory history of Western imperialism, suppression, and exploitation to be overcome, despite the undenied benefits which the West also brought to them. There must be an acceleration in the liquidation of colonialism. A friendly hand must be extended to the peoples who are laboring under the heavy burden of newly won independence, as well as to those who aspire to it. And in that hand must be tangible aid in generous quantity—funds, goods, foodstuffs, equipment, technical assistance. . . .

The United Nations is opposed to imperialism of any kind, ideological or otherwise. The United Nations stands for the freedom and equality of all peoples, irrespective of race, religion, or ideology. It is for the peoples of every society to make their own choices with regard to ideologies, economic systems, and the relationship which is to prevail between the state and the individual. The United Nations is engaged in an historic effort to underwrite the rights of man. It is also attempting to give reassurance to the colonial peoples that their aspirations for freedom can be realized, if only gradually, by peaceful processes.

There can be peace and a better life for all men. Given adequate authority and support, the United Nations can ensure this. But the decision really rests with the peoples of the world. The United Nations belongs to the people, but it is not yet as close to them, as much a part of their conscious interest, as it must come to be. The United Nations must always be on the people's side. Where their fundamental rights and interests are involved, it must never act from mere expediency. At times, perhaps, it has done so, but never to its own advantage nor to that of the sacred causes of peace and freedom. If the peoples of the world are strong in their resolve and if they speak through the United Nations, they need never be confronted with the tragic alternatives of war or dishonorable appeasement, death, or enslavement.

# 24

## SAMUEL COLERIDGE-TAYLOR AND BOOKER T. WASHINGTON

## An Assessment of African and African American Music

### 1904

*The son of a Sierra Leonean father studying medicine in Britain and an English mother, Samuel Coleridge-Taylor (1875–1912) exhibited great musical talent from an early age. The great popularity of his compositions and arrangements in Britain led to triumphal tours of the United States in 1904 and 1906, during which he performed in Boston, New York, and Washington, where he was invited to Theodore Roosevelt's White House. His admiration of Booker T. Washington and W. E. B. Du Bois was reciprocated, and he also collaborated with the African*

Samuel Coleridge-Taylor, *Twenty-four Negro Melodies Transcribed for Piano* (Boston: Oliver Ditson, Company, 1905), viii–x.

*American poet Paul Laurence Dunbar. The second excerpt is from Coleridge-Taylor's foreword to his scores of* Twenty-four Negro Melodies, *in which he places African and African American music in a world context. The first selection is from the introduction to the collection by Booker T. Washington (1856–1915). At that time Washington was the most famous black man in North America. Born in slavery in Virginia, the young Washington made up for the lack of early education and had a distinguished record of academic achievement at Hampton Institute. His educational accomplishments led to his being named the head of the new Tuskegee Institute in Alabama in 1881 at the age of twenty-five; he retained that post until his death. Under Washington, Tuskegee was highly successful in educating black people for careers and became world famous as a symbol of black educational achievement. Washington was awarded honorary degrees by Harvard University (1896) and Dartmouth College (1901). His autobiography,* Up from Slavery, *published in 1901, became a best seller.*

## Washington's Introduction

Negro music is essentially spontaneous. In Africa it sprang into life at the war dance, at funerals, and at marriage festivals. Upon this African foundation the plantation songs of the South were built. According to the testimony of African students at Tuskegee there are in the native African melodies strains that reveal the close relationship between the Negro music of America and Africa, but the imagery and sentiments to which the plantation songs give expression are the outcome of the conditions in America under which the transported children of Africa lived. Wherever companies of Negroes were working together, in the cotton fields and tobacco factories, on the levees and steamboats, on sugar plantations, and chiefly in the fervor of religious gatherings, these melodies sprang into life.

Oftentimes in slavery, as to-day in certain parts of the South, some man or woman with an exceptional voice was paid to lead the singing, the idea being to increase the amount of labor by such singing.

The Negro folk-song has for the Negro race the same value that the folk-song of any other people has for that people. It reminds the race of the "rock whence it was hewn," it fosters race pride, and in the days of slavery it furnished an outlet for the anguish of smitten hearts. The plantation song in America, although an outgrowth of oppression and bondage, contains surprisingly few references to slavery. No race has ever sung so sweetly or with such perfect charity, while looking forward to the "year of Jubilee." The songs abound in Scriptural allusions, and in many instances are unique interpretations of standard hymns.

## Coleridge-Taylor's Foreword

There is a great distinction between the *African* Negro and the *American* Negro Melodies. The African would seem to be more martial and free in character, whereas the American are more personal and tender, though notable exceptions to this rule can be found on either side. One of the most striking points regarding this music is, in the author's opinion, its likeness to that of the Caucasian race. The native music of India, China, and Japan, and in fact all non-European music, is to our more cultivated ears most unsatisfactory, in its monotony and shapelessness. The music of Africa (I am not thinking of American Negro music, which may or may not have felt some white influence) is the great and noteworthy exception. Primitive as it is, it nevertheless has all the elements of the European folk-song and it is remarkable that no alterations have had to be made before treating the Melodies. This is even so with the example from *West* Africa—a highly original number. One conclusion may be safely drawn from this—the Negro is really and truly a most musical personality. What culture may do for the race in this respect has yet to be determined, but the underlying musical nature cannot for a moment be questioned.

## 25

## PAUL ROBESON

## *An African American Appreciation of African Music*

### *1935*

*The son of an African American minister who had run away from slavery, Paul Robeson (1898–1976) grew up in New Jersey and won a scholarship to Rutgers University, from which he graduated in 1911 with distinguished academic and athletic achievements. While attending*

*Paul Robeson Speaks: Writings, Speeches, Interviews, 1918–1974*, ed. Philip S. Foner (New York: Brunner/Mazel Publishers, 1978), 88–91.

*Columbia University Law School, he also became active in the New York theater. Among Robeson's many talents was a magnificent singing voice, which he used in giving the first concert of African American music in 1925. Despite the prevailing racism, the tall, handsome Robeson had a very successful career performing concerts and acting and singing in Broadway plays and Hollywood films. During a prolonged stay in Britain, he became interested in Africa and studied African languages and music. Robeson also became active politically. In 1937 he returned to the United States, where his involvement in civil rights, antifascist, and pro-African organizations brought him under suspicion of the House Un-American Activities Committee. Despite his testimony that he was not a Communist, his passport was revoked from 1950 to 1958. When it was restored, Paul and his wife Eslanda (see Document 32) successfully toured Europe and the Soviet Union until ill health forced him to return to the United States.*

---

I am a Negro. The origin of the Negro is African. It would therefore seem an easy matter for me to assume African nationality.

Instead it is an extremely complicated matter, fraught with the gravest importance to me and some millions of colored folk.

Africa is a Dark Continent not merely because its people are dark-skinned or by reason of its extreme impenetrability, but because its history is lost. We have an amazingly vivid reconstruction of the culture of ancient Egypt, but the roots of almost the whole remainder of Africa are buried in antiquity.

They are, however, rediscoverable; and they will in time be rediscovered.

I am confirmed in this faith by recent researches linking the *culture* of the Negro with that of many peoples of the East.

Let us consider for a moment the problem of my people—the African Negroes in the Occident, and particularly in America.

We are now fourteen millions strong—though perhaps "strong" is not the apt word; for nearly two and a half centuries we were in chains, and although to-day we are technically free and officially labelled "American Citizen," we are at a great economic disadvantage, most trades and many professions being practically barred to us and social barriers inexorably raised.

Consequently the American Negro in general suffers from an acute inferiority complex; it has been drummed into him that the white man is the Salt of the Earth and the Lord of Creation, and as a perfectly natural result his ambition is to become as nearly like a white man as possible.

He is that tragic creature, a man without a nationality. He claims to be American, to be British, to be French—but you cannot assume a nationality as you would a new suit of clothes.

In the country of his adoption, or the country that ruthlessly adopted his forebears, he is an alien; but (herein lies his tragedy) he believes himself to have broken away from his true origins; he has, he argues, nothing whatever in common with the inhabitant of Africa to-day—and that is where I believe he is wrong.

It may be asked "Why disturb him if he is happy in his present state?"

There are two sufficient answers to that; one that he is *not* happy, except in so far as his natural gaiety of disposition overcomes his circumstances—and the fact that a sick man laughs is surely no reason for not attempting to cure his sickness; and the other is that there is a world-necessity above and beyond his immediate needs.

This world-necessity is for an understanding between the nations and peoples which will lead ultimately to the "family of nations" ideal.

To this world-community every nation will contribute whatever it has of culture; and unless the African Negro (including his far-flung collaterals) bestirs himself and comes to a realization of his potentialities and obligations there will be no culture for him to contribute.

At present the younger generation of Negroes in America looks towards Africa and asks "What is there *there* to interest me? What of value has Africa to offer that the Western world cannot give me?"

At first glance the question seems unanswerable. He sees only the savagery, devil-worship, witch-doctors, voo-doo, ignorance, squalor, and darkness taught in American schools.

Where these exist, he is looking at the broken remnants of what was in its day a mighty thing; something which perhaps has not been destroyed, but only driven underground, leaving ugly scars upon the earth's surface to mark the place of its ultimate reappearance. . . .

Mankind is gradually feeling its way back to a more fundamental, more primitive, but perhaps truer religion; and religion, the orientation of man to God or forces greater than himself, must be the basis of all culture.

This religion, this basic culture, has its roots in the Far East, *and in Africa*.

What links the American Negro to this culture? It would take a psycho-anthropologist to give it a name; but its nature is obvious to any earnest inquirer.

Its manifestation occurs in his forms of religion and of art. It has recently been demonstrated beyond a possibility of doubt that the dances, the songs, and the worship perpetuated by the Negro in America are identical with those of his cousins hundreds of years removed in the depths of Africa, whom he has never seen, of whose very existence he is only dimly aware.

His peculiar sense of rhythm alone would stamp him indelibly as African; and a slight variation of this same rhythm-consciousness is to be found among the Tartars and Chinese, to whom he is much more nearly akin than he is to the Arab, for example.

Not long ago I learned to speak Russian, since, the Russians being so closely allied through the Tartars to the Chinese, I expected to find myself more in sympathy with that language than with English, French, or German. I was not disappointed; I found that there were Negro concepts which I could express much more readily in Russian than in other languages.

I would rather sing Russian folk-songs than German grand opera— not because it is necessarily better music, but because it is more *instinctive* and less *reasoned* music. It is in my blood.

The pressing need of the American Negro is an ability to set his own standards. At school, at university, at law school, it didn't matter to me whether white students passed me or I passed them. What mattered was, if I got 85 marks, *why didn't I get* 100? If I got 99, *why didn't I get* 100? "To thine own self be true" is a sentiment sneered at to-day as merely Victorian—but upon its observance may well depend the future of nations and peoples.

It is of course useful and even necessary from an economic and social standpoint for the Negro to *understand* Western ideas and culture, for he will gain nothing by further isolating himself; and I would emphasize that his mere physical return to his place of origin is not the essential condition of his regeneration. In illustration of this take the parallel case of the Jews.

They, like a vast proportion of Negroes, are a race without a nation; but, far from Palestine, they are indissolubly bound by their ancient religious practices—*which they recognize as such*. I emphasize this in contradistinction to the religious practices of the American Negro, which, from the snake-worship practiced in the deep South to the Christianity of the revival meeting, are patently survivals of the earliest African religions; *and he does not recognize them as such*.

Their acknowledgment of their common origin, species, interest, and attitudes binds Jew to Jew; a similar acknowledgment will bind Negro and Negro.

I realize that this will never be accomplished by viewing from afar the dark rites of the witch-doctor—a phenomenon as far divorced from fundamental reality as are the petty bickerings over altar decorations and details of vestment from the intention of Christ.

It may be accomplished, or at least furthered, by patient inquiry. To this end I am learning Swahili, Tivi, and other African dialects—which come easily to me *because their rhythm is the same as that employed by the American Negro in speaking English*; and when the time is ripe I propose to investigate, on the spot, the possibilities of such a regeneration as I have outlined.

Meanwhile in my music, my plays, my films I want to carry always this central idea: to be African.

Multitudes of men have died for less worthy ideals; it is even more eminently worth living for.


# 26

## W. E. B. DU BOIS

# *What Does Africa Mean to Me?*

### *1940 and 1923*

*See the introduction to Document 16 for a biographical overview of Du Bois. In the following essay he recalls his first visit to Liberia and reflects on his changing thinking about race.*

What is Africa to me? Once I should have answered the question simply: I should have said "fatherland" or perhaps better "motherland" because I was born in the century when the walls of race were clear and straight; when the world consisted of mutually exclusive races;

W. E. Burghardt Du Bois, *Dusk of Dawn: An Essay toward an Autobiography of a Race Concept* (New York: Schocken Books, 1968), 116–18, 122–27.

and even though the edges might be blurred, there was no question of exact definition and understanding of the meaning of the word. One of the first pamphlets that I wrote in 1897 was on "The Conservation of Races" wherein I set down as the first article of a proposed racial creed: "We believe that the Negro people as a race have a contribution to make to civilization and humanity which no other race can make."

Since then the concept of race has so changed and presented so much of contradiction that as I face Africa I ask myself: what is it between us that constitutes a tie which I can feel better than I can explain? Africa is, of course, my fatherland. Yet neither my father nor my father's father ever saw Africa or knew its meaning or cared overmuch for it. My mother's folk were closer and yet their direct connection, in culture and race, became tenuous; still, my tie to Africa is strong. On this vast continent were born and lived a large portion of my direct ancestors going back a thousand years or more. The mark of their heritage is upon me in color and hair. These are obvious things, but of little meaning in themselves; only important as they stand for real and more subtle differences from other men. Whether they do or not, I do not know nor does science know today.

But one thing is sure and that is the fact that since the fifteenth century these ancestors of mine and their other descendants have had a common history; have suffered a common disaster and have one long memory. The actual ties of heritage between the individuals of this group, vary with the ancestors that they have in common and many others: Europeans and Semites, perhaps Mongolians, certainly American Indians. But the physical bond is least and the badge of color relatively unimportant save as a badge; the real essence of this kinship is its social heritage of slavery; the discrimination and insult; and this heritage binds together not simply the children of Africa, but extends through yellow Asia and into the South Seas. It is this unity that draws me to Africa.

When shall I forget the night I first set foot on African soil? I am the sixth generation in descent from forefathers who left this land. The moon was at the full and the waters of the Atlantic lay like a lake. All the long slow afternoon as the sun robed herself in her western scarlet with veils of misty cloud, I had seen Africa afar. Cape Mount— that mighty headland with its twin curves, northern sentinel of the realm of Liberia—gathered itself out of the cloud at half past three and then darkened and grew clear. On beyond flowed the dark low undulating land quaint with palm and breaking sea. The world grew black. Africa faded away, the stars stood forth curiously twisted—

Orion in the zenith—the Little Bear asleep and the Southern Cross rising behind the horizon. Then afar, ahead, a lone light shone, straight at the ship's fore. Twinkling lights appeared below, around, and rising shadows. "Monrovia," said the Captain. . . .

As I look back and recall the days, which I have called great—the occasions in which I have taken part and which have had for me and others the widest significance, I can remember none like the first of January, 1924. Once I took my bachelor's degree before a governor, a great college president, and a bishop of New England. But that was rather personal in its memory than in any way epochal. Once before the assembled races of the world I was called to speak in London in place of the suddenly sick Sir Harry Johnston. It was a great hour. But it was not greater than the day when I was presented to the President of the Negro Republic of Liberia.

Liberia had been resting under the shock of world war into which the Allies forced her. She had asked and been promised a loan by the United States to bolster and replace her stricken trade. She had conformed to every preliminary requirement and waited when waiting was almost fatal. It was not simply money, it was world prestige and protection at a time when the little republic was sorely beset by creditors and greedy imperial powers. At the last moment, an insurgent Senate peremptorily and finally refused the request and strong recommendation of President Wilson and his advisers, and the loan was refused. The Department of State made no statement to the world, and Liberia stood naked, not only well-nigh bankrupt, but peculiarly defenseless amid scowling and unbelieving powers.

It was then that the United States made a gesture of courtesy; a little thing, and merely a gesture, but one so unusual that it was epochal. President Coolidge, at the suggestion of William H. Lewis, a leading colored lawyer of Boston, named me, an American Negro traveler, Envoy Extraordinary and Minister Plenipotentiary to Liberia— the highest rank ever given by any country to a diplomatic agent in black Africa. And it named this Envoy the special representative of the President of the United States to the President of Liberia, on the occasion of his inauguration; charging the Envoy with a personal word of encouragement and moral support. It was a significant action. It had in it nothing personal. Another appointee would have been equally significant. But Liberia recognized the meaning. She showered upon the Envoy every mark of appreciation and thanks. The Commander of the Liberian Frontier Force was made his special aide, and a sergeant, his orderly. At ten A.M. New Year's morning, 1924, a company of the

Frontier Force, in red fez and khaki, presented arms before the American Legation and escorted Solomon Porter Hood, the American Minister Resident, and myself as Envoy Extraordinary and my aide to the Presidential Mansion—a beautiful white, verandaed house, waving with palms and fronting a grassy street. . . .

We mounted a broad stairway and into a great room that stretched across the house. Here in semi-circle were ranged the foreign consuls and the cabinet—the former in white, gilt with orders and swords; the latter in solemn black. Present were England, France, Germany, Spain, Belgium, Holland, and Panama, to be presented to me in order of seniority by the small brown Secretary of State with his perfect poise and ease. The President entered—frock-coated with the star and ribbon of a Spanish order on his breast. The American Minister introduced me, and I said:

"The President of the United States has done me the great honor of designating me as his personal representative on the occasion of your inauguration. In so doing, he has had, I am sure, two things in mind. First, he wished publicly and unmistakably to express before the world the interest and solicitude which the hundred million inhabitants of the United States of America have for Liberia. Liberia is a child of the United States, and a sister Republic. Its progress and success is the progress and success of democracy everywhere and for all men; and the United States would view with sorrow and alarm any misfortune which might happen to this Republic and any obstacle that was placed in her path.

"But special and peculiar bonds draw these two lands together. In America live eleven million persons of African descent; they are citizens, legally invested with every right that inheres in American citizenship. And I am sure that in this special mark of the President's favor, he has had in mind the wishes and hopes of Negro Americans. He knows how proud they are of the hundred years of independence which you have maintained by force of arms and by brawn and brain upon the edge of this mighty continent; he knows that in the great battle against color caste in America, the ability of Negroes to rule in Africa has been and ever will be a great and encouraging reenforcement. He knows that the unswerving loyalty of Negro Americans to their country is fitly accompanied by a pride in their race and lineage, a belief in the potency and promise of Negro blood which makes them eager listeners to every whisper of success from Liberia, and eager helpers in every movement for your aid and comfort. In a special sense, the moral burden of Liberia and the advancement and integrity of Liberia is the sincere prayer of America."

And now a word about the African himself—about this primitive black man: I began to notice a truth as I entered southern France. I formulated it in Portugal. I knew it as a great truth one Sunday in Liberia. And the Great Truth was this: efficiency and happiness do not go together in modern culture. Going south from London, as the world darkens it gets happier. . . .

Then we came to the village; how can I describe it? Neither London, nor Paris, nor New York has anything of its delicate, precious beauty. It was a town of the Veys and done in cream and pale purple— still, clean, restrained, tiny, complete. It was no selfish place, but the central abode of fire and hospitality, clean-swept for wayfarers, and best seats were bare. They quite expected visitors, morning, noon, and night; and they gave our hands a quick, soft grasp and talked easily. Their manners were better than those of Park Lane or Park Avenue. Oh, much better and more natural. They showed breeding. The chief's son—tall and slight and speaking good English—had served under the late Colonel Young. He made a little speech of welcome. Long is the history of the Veys and comes down from the Eastern Roman Empire, the great struggle of Islam and the black empires of the Sudan.

We went on to other villages—dun-colored, not so beautiful, but neat and hospitable. In one sat a visiting chief of perhaps fifty years in a derby hat and a robe, and beside him stood a shy young wife done in ebony and soft brown, whose liquid eyes would not meet ours. The chief was taciturn until we spoke of schools. Then he woke suddenly—he had children to "give" to a school. I see the last village fading away; they are plastering the wall of a home, leisurely and carefully. They smiled a good-by—not effusively, with no eagerness, with a simple friendship, as we glided under the cocoa trees and into the silent forest, the gold and silent forest.

And there and elsewhere in two long months I began to learn: primitive men are not following us afar, frantically waving and seeking our goals; primitive men are not behind us in some swift foot-race. Primitive men have already arrived. They are abreast, and in places ahead of us; in others behind. But all their curving advance line is contemporary, not prehistoric. They have used other paths and these paths have led them by scenes sometimes fairer, sometimes uglier than ours, but always toward the Pools of Happiness. Or, to put it otherwise, these folk have the leisure of true aristocracy—leisure for thought and courtesy, leisure for sleep and laughter. They have time for their children—such well-trained, beautiful children with perfect, unhidden bodies. Have you ever met a crowd of children in the east of London or New York, or even on the Avenue at Forty-second or One Hundred and Forty-second Street, and fled to avoid their impudence and utter ignorance of courtesy? Come to Africa, and see well-bred and courteous children, playing happily and never sniffling and whining.

<br>

## 27

## AIMÉ CÉSAIRE

# French West Indian Perspectives on Black Cultural Connections
## 1953

---

*Born on the West Indian island of Martinique to black parents of modest means, Aimé Césaire (1913– ) did well in the local French schools and won a scholarship to study in Paris in 1932. Shortly after his arrival, he became friends with Léopold Senghor of Senegal, whose great intelligence and abilities, Césaire reported, changed his whole image of Africans and opened him to the contemplation of his own African roots. Out of this came his remarkable and celebrated poem, "Cahier d'un retour au pays natal" ("Notebook of a Return to the Native Land"), published in 1939, in which Césaire first used the word négritude to capture his black cultural identity. He lived in Martinique and Haiti during the Second World War, and at its end he was elected to the French Constituent Assembly as a deputy from Martinique and was also elected mayor of the city of Fort-de-France. He was active in the French Communist party. Among his many literary works in this period were a biography of the Haitian revolutionary leader, Toussaint Louverture; a play about Haiti,* The Tragedy of King Christophe; *and a play,* A Season in the Congo,

---

Aimé Césaire, *Discourse on Colonialism*, trans. Joan Pinkham (New York: Monthly Review Press, 1972), 68–75.

*about the first Congo prime minister, Patrice Lumumba. In this 1953*
*interview Césaire discusses the intellectual and literary context of his*
*famous poem.*

Q: I would like to go back to the period in your life in Paris when you
collaborated with Léopold Sédar Senghor and Léon Damas on the
small periodical *L'Etudiant noir*. Was this first stage of the Negritude
expressed in *Return to My Native Land*?

A: Yes, it was already Negritude, as we conceived of it then. There
were two tendencies within our group. On the one hand, there were
people from the left, Communists at that time, such as J. Monnerot,
E. Léro, and René Ménil. They were Communists, and therefore we
supported them. But very soon I had to reproach them—and perhaps
I owe this to Senghor—for being French Communists. There was
nothing to distinguish them either from the French surrealists or from
the French Communists. In other words, their poems were color-
less. . . .

Q: At bottom what separated you from the Communist Martinican
students at that time was the Negro question.

A: Yes, the Negro question. At that time I criticized the Communists for forgetting our Negro characteristics. They acted like Communists, which was all right, but they acted like abstract Communists. I
maintained that the political question could not do away with our condition as Negroes. We are Negroes, with a great number of historical
peculiarities. I suppose that I must have been influenced by Senghor
in this. At the time I knew absolutely nothing about Africa. Soon after-
ward I met Senghor, and he told me a great deal about Africa. He
made an enormous impression on me: I am indebted to him for the
revelation of Africa and African singularity. And I tried to develop a
theory to encompass all of my reality. . . .

Q: How do you explain the emergence, in the years between the
two world wars, of these parallel movements—in Haiti, the United
States, Cuba, Brazil, Martinique, etc.—that recognized the cultural
particularities of Africa?

A: I believe that at that time in the history of the world there was a
coming to consciousness among Negroes, and this manifested itself in
movements that had no relationship to each other.

Q: There was the extraordinary phenomenon of jazz.

A: Yes, there was the phenomenon of jazz. There was the Marcus

Garvey movement. I remember very well that even when I was a child I had heard people speak of Garvey. . . .

He inspired a mass movement, and for several years he was a symbol to American Negroes. In France there was a newspaper called *Le Cri des nègres*. . . .

I remember very well that around that time we read the poems of Langston Hughes and Claude McKay. I knew very well who McKay was because in 1929 or 1930 an anthology of American Negro poetry appeared in Paris. And McKay's novel, *Banjo*—describing the life of dock workers in Marseilles—was published in 1930. This was really one of the first works in which an author spoke of the Negro and gave him a certain literary dignity. I must say, therefore, that although I was not directly influenced by any American Negroes, at least I felt that the movement in the United States created an atmosphere that was indispensable for a very clear coming to consciousness. During the 1920's and 1930's I came under three main influences, roughly speaking. The first was the French literary influence, through the works of Mallarmé, Rimbaud, Lautréamont, and Claudel. The second was Africa. I knew very little about Africa, but I deepened my knowledge through ethnographic studies. . . .

And as for the third influence, it was the Negro Renaissance Movement in the United States, which did not influence me directly but still created an atmosphere which allowed me to become conscious of the solidarity of the black world. . . .

Q: How would you describe your encounter with Senghor, the encounter between Antillean Negritude and African Negritude? Was it the result of a particular event or of a parallel development of consciousness?

A: It was simply that in Paris at that time there were a few dozen Negroes of diverse origins. There were Africans, like Senghor, Guianans, Haitians, North Americans, Antilleans, etc. This was very important for me.

Q: In this circle of Negroes in Paris, was there a consciousness of the importance of African culture?

A: Yes, as well as an awareness of the solidarity among blacks. We had come from different parts of the world. It was our first meeting. We were discovering ourselves. This was very important.

Q: It was extraordinarily important. How did you come to develop the concept of Negritude?

A: I have a feeling that it was somewhat of a collective creation. I used the term first, that's true. But it's possible we talked about it in our group. It was really a resistance to the politics of assimilation. Until that time, until my generation, the French and the English—but especially the French—had followed the politics of assimilation unrestrainedly. We didn't know what Africa was. Europeans despised everything about Africa, and in France people spoke of a civilized world and a barbarian world. The barbarian world was Africa, and the civilized world was Europe. Therefore the best thing one could do with an African was to assimilate him: the ideal was to turn him into a Frenchman with black skin. . . .

Q: It was a case of total alienation.

A: I think you've put your finger on it. Our struggle was a struggle against alienation. That struggle gave birth to Negritude. Because Antilleans were ashamed of being Negroes, they searched for all sorts of euphemisms for Negro: they would say a man of color, a dark-complexioned man, and other idiocies like that. . . .

That's when we adopted the word *nègre*, as a term of defiance. It was a defiant name. To some extent it was a reaction of enraged youth. Since there was shame about the word *nègre*, we chose the word *nègre*. I must say that when we founded *L'Etudiant noir*, I really wanted to call it *L'Etudiant nègre*, but there was a great resistance to that among the Antilleans.

Q: Some thought that the word *nègre* was offensive.

A: Yes, too offensive, too aggressive, and then I took the liberty of speaking of *négritude*. There was in us a defiant will, and we found a violent affirmation in the words *nègre* and *négritude*.

Q: In *Return to My Native Land* you have stated that Haiti was the cradle of Negritude. In your words, "Haiti, where Negritude stood on its feet for the first time." Then, in your opinion, the history of our country is in a certain sense the prehistory of Negritude. How have you applied the concept of Negritude to the history of Haiti?

A: Well, after my discovery of the North American Negro and my discovery of Africa, I went on to explore the totality of the black world, and that is how I came upon the history of Haiti. I love Martinique, but it is an alienated land, while Haiti represented for me the heroic Antilles, the African Antilles. I began to make connections between the Antilles and Africa, and Haiti is the most African of the Antilles. It is at the same time a country with a marvelous history: the first Negro epic of the New World was written by Haitians, people like Toussaint l'Ouverture, Henri Christophe, Jean-Jacques Dessalines, etc. Haiti is not very well known in Martinique. I am one of the few Martinicans who know and love Haiti.

Q: Then for you the first independence struggle in Haiti was a confirmation, a demonstration of the concept of Negritude. Our national history is Negritude in action.

A: Yes, Negritude in action. Haiti is the country where Negro people stood up for the first time, affirming their determination to shape a new world, a free world.

# 28

## LÉOPOLD SÉDAR SENGHOR

# A Defense of Négritude

## 1966

*After attending Catholic mission schools in the Senegal colony of French West Africa, Léopold Sédar Senghor (1906–2001) won a scholarship to study in Paris. He was the first black African to receive a diploma from the Sorbonne. He taught in France during the 1930s and was very active in intellectual and black literary circles, working with Aimé Césaire among others and reading the literature of the Harlem Renaissance. He served in the French army in World War II, was a prisoner of war, and was active in the French Resistance movement. In 1945 he was elected to the French Assembly as a deputy from Senegal, serving until 1958. During this time he also established himself as a leading poet and intellectual. His poems are regularly included in anthologies of modern French poetry. In 1983 he was elected to the French Academy. When the French empire in Africa was thrown into crisis by the British steps to give independence to their West African colonies, Senghor became a political activist. In 1960 he was elected president of Senegal, a post that he held until 1980. In this essay he reflects on the different meanings of the word* négritude, *which Césaire had coined, and the relationship of a uniquely black cultural identity to membership in global humanity.*

"Négritude et la civilisation de l'universel," an address given at the University of Beirut, May 19, 1966, 69–70, 74–75, 78–79, in Léopold Sédar Senghor, *Liberté III: Négritude et civilisation de l'universel*, trans. David Northrup (Paris: Editions du Seuil, 1977).

## Négritude Is a Twentieth-Century Humanism

For the thirty odd years that we have been proclaiming Négritude, some have regularly accused us of racism. These same people sometimes assert that "Négritude is an inferiority complex." Now the same word cannot, without contradiction, signify "racism" and "inferiority complex."

No, Négritude is nothing of the sort. It is neither racism nor self-negation. It is rooted in the self and self-confirming—in one's very being. Négritude is nothing other than the *African personality* of English-speaking Negro-Africans. Nothing other than this "black personality" discovered and proclaimed by the American *New Negro* movement. As Langston Hughes wrote in a proclamation just after the First World War: "We . . . who create now intend to express our individual dark-skinned selves without fear or shame. . . . We know we are beautiful. And ugly too. The tom-tom cries and the tom-tom laughs."[2] Perhaps our only originality in the matter is to have tried to define the concept rigorously: to have wished to elaborate it as a weapon, an instrument of liberation and a contribution to twentieth-century humanism.

But what is Négritude? Ethnologists and sociologists speak these days of "different civilizations." There is evidence that peoples are different in their ideas and their languages, their philosophies and their religions, their morals and their institutions, their literatures and their arts. Who would deny that Negro-African peoples also have a certain manner of conceiving life and living? Likely no one, for otherwise one would not speak of "Negro art" for the last sixty years, and black Africa would be today the only continent without ethnologists and sociologists. So then, what is Négritude? It is *the ensemble of the values of the black world's civilization*, that is, a certain active presence in the world—in the universe. It is, as John Reed and Clive Wake say,[3] a certain "way of relating oneself to the world and to others." Yes, it is essentially relation with and movement toward the world, contact and

---

[2]Langston Hughes (1902–1967) was a major poet of the Harlem Renaissance. Senghor quotes this in French. The translation restores Hughes's original words from "The Negro Artist and the Racial Mountain," published in *The Nation* in 1926. [Ed.]

[3]John Reed and Clive Wake, two young white instructors at University College, Salisbury, Southern Rhodesia, who selected and translated Léopold Sédar Senghor's *Prose and Poetry* (London: Oxford University Press, 1965). The phrase Senghor cites in English does not appear in their introduction to that work. [Ed.]

participation with others. Because of that, Négritude is today necessary to the world; it is a twentieth-century humanism. . . .

Ethnologists have often vaunted the unity, equilibrium, and harmony of Negro-African civilization—of black society, *communalist* but personalist, where, because founded on dialogue and the reciprocity of services, the group surpassed the individual without overwhelming him, because it allowed him to develop as a *person*. I would like to underline how much these traits of Négritude permit it to be inserted in contemporary humanism, permitting black Africa to make its contribution to Universal Civilization, which is needed by the fragmented but interdependent world of the second half of the twentieth century. And first, on international cooperation, which must be, which will be the cornerstone of that civilization. It is thanks to these virtues of Négritude that decolonization was accomplished south of the Sahara without too much bloodshed or hatred, that a positive cooperation, founded "on dialogue and the reciprocity of services" was set up between the former colonists and former colonized, that a new spirit breathed at the UN, where "no" votes and fist banging on the table are no longer signs of power. Thanks to these virtues, peaceful cooperation can be extended to South Africa, Southern Rhodesia, and the Portuguese colonies, if the Manichean spirit of the Albo-Europeans should want to be open to dialogue. . . .

A final proof that Négritude may be a twentieth-century humanism is furnished by the welcome the world gave to the First World Festival of Negro (Nègre) Arts held in Dakar [Senegal] from April 1st to 24th, 1966. The great nations of Europe and America participated by sending either works from their collections or, in the case of the United States of America and Brazil, their black artists. It is significant that the "Arab" states of Africa were represented at Dakar. . . .

In any case, the twentieth-century Negro (Nègre), the New Negro . . . intends to contribute doubly to Universal Civilization: to the twentieth-century civilization. On the one hand, by bringing the richness of its philosophy, its literature, and its traditional art; on the other hand, by showing the loans it has made since the Renaissance to other civilizations, particularly the European and the Arabo-Berber. That was precisely the object of the First World Festival of Negro Arts: the demonstration of twentieth-century humanism.

# 5
# Transatlantic Voyagers, 1914–1963

## 29

## JAMES E. KWEGYIR AGGREY

## *A Gold Coast African in America*

### *1914*

*Born in the British colony of the Gold Coast, James Aggrey (1875–1927) was driven by a passionate love of learning and Christianity. He completed his mission-school education in record time and taught in mission schools until 1898, when he went to the United States and enrolled in Livingstone College, an African Methodist Episcopal Zion Church institution in North Carolina, from which he earned a B.A. in 1902. After serving for several years as a member of Livingstone's faculty, Aggrey's passion for more education drove him to enroll in Columbia University, where he began work on a doctorate. His talents and drive, well illustrated in the following letter to W. J. Trent, his close friend and later principal of Livingstone, also attracted the attention of the Phelps-Stokes Fund, a charitable trust dedicated to promoting "the education of Negroes, both in Africa and the United States." He served on two important commissions for the Phelps-Stokes Fund in Africa in 1920 and 1924. Aggrey returned to the Gold Coast to accept a senior position in a prestigious school but died suddenly while on leave in New York City completing his dissertation. He was an inspiration to many.*

Quoted in Edwin W. Smith, *Aggrey of Africa: A Study in Black and White* (New York: For the Phelps-Stokes Fund by the Friendship Press, 1929), 102–5.

I did succeed in getting to New York and in entering Columbia once more. The very ground felt sacred, and I determined to make good, in spite of odds against me. . . . I borrowed 75 dollars and came on. . . . My registration expenses, rather tuition, cost me exactly 50 dollars. It would have cost fifty-five, but being an old student of Columbia they cut off five. So I paid fifty dollars for tuition in Educational Psychology . . . in Spanish, and in General Seminar Course in Sociology. . . . It cost me in all not less than 10 dollars a week for board and room rent, and car fares and laundry, sometimes more. Besides these I had to keep up my home and family in Salisbury. Add all this together, then put on top of them the books I had to buy and you can imagine, with my railroad expenses here, my expenses. I had to leave my house soon after 7.30 in order to get to Columbia by 8.15, as the lectures in Educational Psychology began then. I was in school until after 2.30— had a class from 8.15 to 9.15, from 9.30 to 10.30, from 10.30 to 11.30, then from 1.0 to 2.30. I hurried up a lunch or dinner at the University commons, and either studied until evening or came home to 136th Street by almost a circuitous route, and either got ready to fill a preaching or speaking engagement or visited places for sociological studies. Mind you I had to study for four classes, and in two of them I had to carry work done every day. Well, I was here, and I was not going to say "die." I preached or spoke almost—rather, practically— every Sunday, sometimes twice, sometimes thrice a Sunday. . . . I have preached both in white churches and colored; have spoken to Methodists, Congregationalists, and Moravians, and have addressed both the Y.M. and the Y.W.C.A. Sunday afternoon gatherings.

I had to make good if I died in the doing—and Heaven sustained me. . . . I had to work. Often I would go to bed at 3 A.M., more often at 2, never before 12 or 1, and get up at 5.30 A.M., and would be studying or going to school, or doing research work, or hustling for money. Do you understand now why I could not write you the letter I wanted to? . . .

Well, in Spanish I can now read the beautiful works of Cervantes, such as *Don Quixote*, in the original. We finished two books in Spanish. . . . I took the two courses, one in the morning and one in the afternoon, in Educational Psychology and the Diagnosis and Treatment of atypical children. We visited Rendall's Island—examined morons, imbeciles, idiots, epileptics, and other grades of mental troubles. . . . I was the only colored in all my classes. But I was right there with them. . . .

Well, in examination, F is failure, D is pass, C is good, B is very good,

A is excellent. You may be glad to learn that in spite of all the hindrances I made A in all my examinations, and in some had public honorable mention, although the only colored in the class. I made good. . . .

Of course I can talk freely to you. The general seminar course was open only to post-graduate students. There were only eleven of us in that—four ladies, and seven gentlemen, and of the seven one a Negro. I think all the young women were M.A.'s, and several of the men too. One of them was a Bachelor of Science from Wesleyan University, all working for the Master's or Doctor's degree, most of them for the Ph.D. Well, in our tabulation report work, one day I discovered there were southerners in the class, and even among the northerners there was objection to a colored man being admitted (if they were asked to vote) to white Social Clubs. That was a chance for me to discuss the race question from a sociological point of view. I served notice, and when the day came I held forth. It was an open parliament. I made no enemy, but rather friends, and Dr. [Franklin Henry] Giddings made me a great compliment before the whole class. I said, I am going back South to teach Sociology, and if my views were untruths I was willing to be corrected. I did not want sentiment, but sense, not fiction, but fact, not prejudice and superstition but conclusions arrived at through logical deductions and inductions based on tenable premises. Well, sir, you ought to have been there. The period was fifty minutes for the whole recitation. . . . Dr. Giddings, before I had spoken ten minutes, halted me and paid me the compliment and told the class that from what he had learned from conversation with me, and what Dr. Jones had told him, I was fully able to answer all questions, that I had had ample opportunities to study the Race question from a very important angle—even more advantageous than those of DuBois and Washington, etc., etc., and that any in the class was permitted to ask questions. . . . I cannot tell it all. Dr. Giddings agreed with me, and we all decided that it is either through fear or ignorance that the colored is mistreated. They asked me what I thought would be the best way of solving the problem. I said, the southern white man can do most to solve it. Giddings agreed with me *in toto*, and told the southerners in the class to go back after that speech and start the ball rolling for better affairs. Ever after that I was a lion in the kindliness of all. I won them all. One classmate, Rev. W. H. Sutton, asked me to go and preach for him. I went and preached twice and lectured once.

Well, after the session closed, Dr. Giddings called me to his private office and made me feel real good. In our work in the class in experimentations proving or disproving Consciousness of Kind, without consulting anybody all through the session it was discovered that four of the eleven of us agreed oftenest in tastes, in ideas of what is the best thing to do, and in recognition of the things of supreme interest. Those four were, to quote Dr. Giddings, one colored man, one Jewess, and two white men of Anglo-Saxon lineage, and, strange to say, one a Northerner and one a Southerner—proving conclusively Consciousness of Kind. We enjoyed our studies very much.

Then another: Between examinations I paused long enough to write a Latin poem for the *Columbia Student.* . . . Dr. Giddings read it, complimented me before the whole class, then asked me to read it. I read and put the sentiments into English, and I was uproariously cheered by the whole class, a Southerner being the first to rise to my seat and shake my hand in congratulations; all congratulated me, thanked me, and said they were going to get copies to keep. That was the last day and we bade each other good-bye. Lots of nice things were said to me by all my class-mates. As I began to say, Dr. Giddings called me into his private office and there again reiterated the nice things he had been saying before the class. He wants me to come back next summer, to make Sociology my major study. . . . So I am going to come back next summer if I live and continue till I get through in Sociology, Economics, and another study. . . . Pray for me, Zeus, that I may be always humble and allow God to use me.

## 30

### NNAMDI AZIKIWE

# A Nigerian in America

## 1925–1933

*Born to Igbo parents, Nnamdi Azikiwe (1904–1996) grew up in Northern Nigeria, where his father was a civil servant. After attending Catholic and Protestant mission boarding schools in his home area, he resolved to continue his education in the United States, first by a foiled*

Nnamdi Azikiwe, *My Odyssey: An Autobiography* (New York: Praeger Publishers), 116–22, 129–30, 136, 147, 157–59. © 1970 in London, England, by Nnamdi Azikiwe.

*attempt to stow away and then in 1925 with his passage paid from his father's meager savings. In the United States he attended the traditionally black Storer College, Howard University, and Lincoln University, as well as Columbia University and the University of Pennsylvania, paying his costs with money earned as a laborer and from scholarships. By 1930 Ben Zik, as he called himself in the United States, earned a string of degrees in political science, anthropology, and journalism. After returning to Nigeria, he started an influential newspaper, the* West African Pilot, *in 1937 and co-founded (with Herbert Macaulay, Bishop Crowther's grandson) Nigeria's first national political party in 1944. Azikiwe was a key leader in the independence movement, served as the first African premier of Eastern Nigeria, the first governor-general of the independent Federation of Nigeria, and the first president of the Federal Republic of Nigeria. Overthrown in a military coup in 1966, he supported the breakaway Republic of Biafra in its unsuccessful effort to become a separate country. Azikiwe reconciled himself and was active in Nigerian educational and political life until his death.*

I scored "A" and "B" in all my studies excepting in Psychology where I made "C" and in Education, where a Negro woman teacher, who impressed me as a psychological problem, gave me the only "D" in my whole academic career in the United States. Of course, I do not, by this, mean to discredit female teachers, because the majority of the "A" grades I made at Storer College were awarded to me by white and black female teachers, although the subjects were in the sciences and ancient language, where one either knows or one does not know, unlike certain courses where opinions vary and conflict, and one is at the mercy of the prejudices of a particular teacher.

My studies in political science gave me the necessary background for my life's work. I remember Professor Tunnell's regular joke that why Negroes failed to resist injustice actively was because they were too fond of "eating pork chops"; in other words, the easy life. Because of this joke, we used to call him "Pork Chop" Tunnell. But we learned from him the need to organize resistance to political misrule, which implied hard work and personal sacrifice on the part of the organizers.

Another lesson we learned from this veteran professor, who was said to have hailed originally from the Caribbean, was the necessity to arouse underprivileged people from their attitude of lethargy and nonchalance towards their lot. Freedom was a universal gift, he would assert; therefore, it was a birthright of humanity of which the Negro was a co-inheritor.

When Professor [Ralph] Bunche took over, we embarked on the struggle for individual freedom and for the enthronement of the rule of law throughout the earth. With me, this meant that I must value my personal liberty, as far as expression, movement, privacy, and safety are concerned. It also meant that the conduct of the constituted authorities should be guided by the canons of written law, a contravention of which should nullify their official acts and make them illegal.

Contact with Professor [William Leo] Hansberry opened a new world to me. This modest and self-effacing scholar assumed the task of venturing into a new frontier of human knowledge. Because he was a generation ahead of his time, coupled with the inferiority complex that was inherent in the environment in which he thrived, his life's work was not appreciated, and the university he worked for failed to carve a niche for itself in a field which is now exploited to the full by the leading American institutions of higher learning.

Professor Hansberry's courses in anthropology covered both physical and cultural aspects. He taught us the biological origins of the human species, illustrating his themes with priceless incursions into anthropological literature. This Negro scholar simplified to us the theses of Blumenbach and other pioneer scholars of anthropology and their contributions to learning. His explanations of how the factors of historical geology affected the evolution of man were most thrilling and fascinating. We were able to appreciate why Charles Darwin correctly thought that Africa was the cradle of the human race. . . .

Professor Hansberry's exposition of the concept of race, language, and culture was a paragon of simplicity. We were able to appreciate the main racial divisions of mankind, their peculiarities, their distribution on the face of the earth, and the scientific attitude to race, in comparison with the pseudo-scientific views of certain "racial" anthropologists, fathered by Gobineau and his satellites. He taught us the fallacy of wrongly mixing racial with linguistic and cultural factors. He made us read what matured scholars like Boas, Sapir, and others were thinking on these lines.

Finally, this humble teacher linked his researches in anthropology with the origins of African history. He offered courses to show the role of persons of African descent in ancient, medieval, and modern history. He delved into the depths of Egyptology to appreciate what such names as Piankhi and Tirhaka meant to the xxvth dynasty of ancient Egypt. He emphasized the humanitarian influence of Ethiopian warriors, and demonstrated how it might have affected the development of the international law of war. Then he opened a new world to us in medieval history, pinpointing the role of Ghana, Mali, Melle, and Songhay in the history of Africa. . . .

My studies in economics were concerned mainly with the effect of economic forces on the development of human personality. The emphasis in my courses was not so much on descriptive and analytical economics as on its applied forms, particularly the struggle between capital and labor, the exercise by workers of the fundamental freedom of association, the right of collective bargaining, and the ethics of the great economic systems of the world. Having been a menial worker and having associated with the unskilled workers of America, I absorbed Professor [Abraham L.] Harris's lectures and did not hesitate to follow through with a number of irritating questions in his office after class hours.

My courses in philosophy were under Professor [Alain LeRoy] Locke. He had just published *The New Negro* and he was sought after by many organizations to tell them the good news. His classroom lectures were usually dry but the substance was meaty. By delving into the various schools of philosophy I was convinced that although the western system was more systematic than the African, nevertheless African philosophy was practical in the sense that people did not waste time on logic and frivolous arguments. Their philosophy was more pragmatic in that it was related to the practical problems of every day life which they solved by adapting themselves to the logic of reason and experience.

Howard University gave me an insight into the biological origins of human behavior. I took a course in psychology for fun; but I found it most instructive because it introduced me to Watson's thesis on behaviorism. Although I had opportunity to know the essentials of the other schools of thought in this fascinating field of study, I have since become a behaviorist. My keen interest in biology is probably responsible for this prejudice.

In the field of sociology, I decided to duplicate Aggrey's experience. Apart from the principles of sociology, I delved into its other facets, like social psychology, social pathology (crime, prostitution, poverty), criminology, penology, the race problem, municipal sociology, rural sociology, etc. My conclusion was that the society in which we live must be treated like an individual to prevent it from becoming a victim of pathological factors. If we had crime, it was not because people necessarily were criminally inclined; faulty social organization was mainly responsible. The same applied to prostitution and poverty. On the race problem, it was obvious that attitudes must be changed and compromises effected, otherwise society was bound to face upheavals. . . .

I had not made enough money to return to Howard so I decided to proceed to Tuskegee Institute and study the art and science of printing. I filled the application form and booked my ticket from New York to Tuskegee. Since my personal belongings were left in Washington, I decided to break my journey there. On arrival in Washington I went to Cyril[1] and told him my plight. I also informed him that I must leave Howard University due to my being financially embarrassed.

Cyril demonstrated to me one peculiar trait of the West Indian which is ennobling: humanitarianism. He had learned to regard me as his brother and he could not, he pleaded, see me leave Howard University for financial reasons. Cyril begged that I should give him three hours and he would see what could be done. I insisted that if he failed to return within three hours I would be on my way to Alabama, for I had telegraphed the Tuskegee authorities to expect me.

About an hour later, Professor Locke came to the International House with Cyril. After a few minutes' discussion, Dr. Locke said that he needed an assistant who understood typing and office management. He was prepared to pay 25 dollars monthly to any student who would do the work satisfactorily, and the hours of work would be three hours daily, either from 4 to 7 P.M. or from 5 to 8 P.M.

I assured him that I could type fairly well and that I could handle his correspondence creditably, although I was not familiar with the use of the dictaphone, with which he used to dictate articles or letters when he felt like doing so and his secretary was away. This changed my plans, and also changed my life's career for, by coming into personal contact with Dr. Locke, I was able to drink from the deep fountain of his almost limitless knowledge. . . .

Immediately after the end of the first semester, I was awarded a scholarship by the Phelps–Stokes Fund which made it possible for me to pay for the rest of the school year and have some money for the summer.

Dr. Locke was largely instrumental in securing this scholarship for me. During my typing service at Dr. Locke's residence at 1326 R Street NW, I was able to appreciate the versatility of this scholar and his penchant for making friends, one of whom was Dr. Joseph Boakye

[1]Cyril Olliviere, a Howard medical student. [Ed.]

Danquah, the first West African to earn the degree of doctor of philosophy from the University of London. . . .

The 'twenties and early 'thirties saw the emergence of the New Negro movement in the United States, which subsequently took the shape of a new Africa movement in the continent of Africa. This was due to a fermentation of ideas among scholars, intellectuals, writers, artists, and politicians who sought for fair play and improved living conditions for the underprivileged people of African descent in all the lands of the earth. There were some pertinent reasons for this upsurge.

World War I had recently ended. While American intervention helped to swing the balance in favor of the Allied powers, yet the slogan which President Woodrow Wilson, the professor-turned-statesman, emblazoned to mankind was "to make the world safe for democracy." After the Treaty of Versailles, the Central Powers were thoroughly discredited and humiliated. The principle of self-determination had given birth to new members in the family of nations, who took their places in the League of Nations under the panoply of collective security.

The colored races realized that their lot was the back-seat. Japan became involved in the race to become a world power, following its industrial revolution. China was involved in an internal convulsion which took two decades to settle; indeed it is a divided country today. The remaining parts of Asia and Africa were the footstools of the victorious powers, who now planned how to divide the spoils of war, the Americans finding a convenient shelter under the roof of isolationism.

Marcus Garvey published his *Philosophy and Opinions* and thus struck the first blow for a new Africa that would be politically-minded. Kwegyir Aggrey confined his ideas to the need for a social rebirth and a new spiritual outlook among and towards the Africans. Some African leaders, such as Casely Hayford, Herbert Macaulay, Bankole Bright, and E. F. Small, prepared a blueprint for the post-war era. But it was left to the American Negro, who played a no less glorious role in the various theaters of the World War I than his white compatriot, to articulate for a renaissance in thought and in action, as far as Negroes were concerned in the United States. Among the leaders of thought in this movement were Garvey, DuBois, Locke, Moton, Kelly Miller, and Kerlin.

The National Congress of British West Africa made its presence felt under the prudent guidance of Casely Hayford of the Gold Coast, although he had to die broken-hearted because a new generation of

Gold Coasters emerged and, like Pharaoh of old, knew not Joseph—and so thoroughly discredited this happy warrior of the 'twenties. Garvey founded the Universal Negro Improvement Association determined to rouse the racial consciousness of black people everywhere. He succeeded in many ways, especially among the masses. DuBois concentrated among intellectuals and started the Pan-African Movement in the attempt to co-ordinate the nationalist crusade for freedom in Africa.

In the United States itself, Kelly Miller published *The Everlasting Stain*; Kerlin published *Negro Poets and Their Poems*, turning the searchlight of critical opinion on the hitherto untapped literature of protest written by Negro poets. Then Alain Locke published *The New Negro*, which was a collection of the writings of Negro poets, dramatists, novelists, painters, and sculptors, reflecting the mood of the articulate section of the American *literati*.

Miller and Locke taught at Howard University, whilst Kerlin taught at Lincoln University. Both universities became centers of a dynamic movement of thought for the rehabilitation of people of African descent. Langston Hughes, who graduated from Lincoln University in 1929, had published *The Weary Blues*; while Countee Cullen published *Colour* after studying at Harvard University. This literature of protest at the lot of the American Negro altered the attitude of those who had been taught to take the Negro for granted. It laid the foundation for the resistance movements of the 'forties, 'fifties, and 'sixties.

As a young student, I was naturally affected by this intellectual ferment. Although I did not study under Professor Kelly Miller, yet I read his articles which were published weekly in the *Norfolk Journal and Guide* and other Aframerican newspapers. I have already explained my contacts with Dr. Locke. The way these protests affected those of us who were putting finishing touches to our studies, both in the United States and in the United Kingdom, is material here, because it laid a solid foundation for the life work of so many of us. . . .

Founded in 1854 as Ashmun Institute, Lincoln University is a private institution operated under the auspices of the Presbyterian Church, although it is partly subsidized by the State of Pennsylvania. . . .

Based on my transcript and due to my desire to graduate in June 1930, I was placed in the senior class; but there was doubt whether I would be able to do the required extraordinary studies so as to be able to satisfy all the requirements for graduation. I studied hard and, at the end of the first semester, I was able to rank in the first group on the class roll. This also entitled me to a special scholarship.

Life at a men's institution was different from that at Howard University, which was co-educational. The "bull sessions" at Lincoln University maintained the same intensity as was the case in Washington, but the boys at Lincoln were famous for their ability to "woof," not minding whether they were loud and wrong. At times it became a matter of who made the loudest noise, interspersed with solid argumentation. Some of my class-mates were in the front rank of scholarship, but when it came to "bull sessions" they did not allow themselves to be out-woofed by anybody.

Our class president was Professor W. T. V. Fontaine, who made history by piercing through the color barrier to become one of the first persons of African descent to be appointed Associate Professor of Philosophy at the University of Pennsylvania. "Footney," as we called him, was one of the prized students of Dean Johnson's philosophy class. After leaving Lincoln he earned his master's degree and the doctorate at that Quaker institution. He and my anthropology teacher at Penn, Professor A. I. Hallowell, were delegated by the University of Pennsylvania to represent it during my inauguration as Governor-General of Nigeria in November 1960.

The other product of our "bull sessions" who, like the rest of us, has also "bulled" his way to the top, was Thurgood Marshall, who made history in the desegregation case before the United States Supreme Court in 1954. As special counsel of the National Association for the Advancement of Colored People (NAACP), Thurgood hardly realized that in thirteen years he would adorn the highest judicial bench of America. Yet he got his early practice in the "bull sessions" at Lincoln. In 1954, when Howard University honored both of us by conferring on us the honorary doctorate degree in law, we sat next to each other at the special dinner arranged for that occasion. Unlike our experience at Lincoln a quarter of a century earlier, our table manners were impeccable. . . .

After I obtained the MA and the M SC degrees, Lincoln University confirmed my appointment from part-time instructorship to full-time. So in the fall of 1933 I worked full time and had to devote my leisure exclusively to teaching. Because some of the professors were on sabbatical leave, I had to "pinch hit" for them, especially in the department of history, where I offered general courses in ancient, medieval, modern, and English history and African history. The last course almost caused an uproar at Lincoln University, because some of the professors felt that the African had no history worthy of academic attention.

In response, I prepared a syllabus for African history and demonstrated the rich literature that was available in this field, thanks to the pioneering researches of Professor Hansberry of Howard University, Dr. Woodson, W. H. Ferris, J. A. Rogers, and others. I persuaded the authorities of Lincoln University to invite Hansberry to come and lecture our congregation on "African Historiography from Ancient to Contemporary Times." It was an original lecture and it opened the eyes of many to the possibilities of African history and its affinity with the origins of the American Negro.

The life of a university instructor is almost ideal, especially to a young man or woman with literary taste and aptitude. One comes into contact with youths and older people of different temperaments, ideas, and outlooks, who are uniformly ambitious to make a mark for themselves in the world. I noted that some of the young matriculants, after spending a year or two at Lincoln University, became intelligently articulate and forceful in their expression, manner, and quest for social justice, and I realized why university education anywhere enables an individual to discover himself.

Noticing how students of African descent, American, British, or otherwise by nationality, were ignorant of their past, it dawned upon me that research into the origins and development of the African in the stream of world history should be a definite contribution to the field of learning. So I intensified my research on "the African in History." Whenever I was not engaged in lecturing to my classes, I was busy doing research on Liberian diplomatic history on the one hand, and probing the dark mist which hung over the history of African peoples on the other. . . .

I thought of the opportunities I would have in America if I obtained the PhD and had a lifelong job of teaching and inspiring young people, rubbing shoulders with the best brains of the world, and hobnobbing in the academic cloister. I also thought of the difficulties facing my people in Africa: their inability to appreciate their unlimited opportunities; their ignorance of their latent giant's strength; and their innocence of the fact that their homeland seemed to them a paradise contrasted with the homeland of their rulers who lived in the temperate zones, where life was one continuous struggle for existence and survival.

# 31

## CONSTANCE HORTON CUMMINGS-JOHN

# A Sierra Leonean in America

### 1936, 1945–1951

*Constance Horton (1918–2000) came from an elite Sierra Leonean family. She attended Freetown's best schools and continued her education in London. In 1936 she accepted an invitation to study in the United States, where, as she describes in the first selection here, she was struck by Americans' racism and by their ignorance about Africa. Back in Freetown in 1937 she married Ethan Cummings-John (who later became ambassador to Liberia), accepted an appointment as principal of an AME girls' school, and won election to the Freetown municipal council on a radical nationalist ticket. In the second selection this remarkable woman describes her Pan-African activities in the United States after World War II. The Sierra Leone Women's Movement, which she founded in 1951, was prominent in Sierra Leone's struggle for independence.*

The first place on my itinerary was Cornell University where I took courses in education, home economics, and colonial problems. I talked to many American students. That was how I started to see the way in which Africa was really misrepresented, how Americans did not consider Africans as normal human beings. Over there the missionaries presented us as half human. People said all kinds of things to me: "Please show us your tail; please let us see this or that about you; tell us something about the wild animals and how you all roam the streets together; tell us if you are afraid of the lions and leopards and tigers at home in your village."

I tried to explain to them about Africa because I had travelled to places other than Sierra Leone. I had been to the Gold Coast and a few other places, so I had seen a bit of Africa. My family spread all the

Constance Agatha Cummings-John, *Memoirs of a Krio Leader*, ed. LaRay Denzer (Ibadan, Nigeria: Sam Bookman for Humanities Research Center, 1995), 25, 29, 34, 35, 64, 68–69.

way down the coast from Sierra Leone to San Thome, Angola, and Fernando Po. For decades my people had been going back and from all those places. I knew that all these stories that I now heard were cooked up, so I explained to them exactly what Sierra Leone was and what life was like there. These explanations produced even more questions. They wanted to know where I learned my English, what language I spoke at home, how I managed in Africa, were there other people like myself there. Some of them even doubted that I came from there. They disputed my claim, maintaining, "You can't be an African. You must have come from the West Indies or from England. You don't look or sound like the Africans that we hear about." . . .

Because I was studying the Jeanes School system, I travelled in the South to observe black colleges that employed it. When it came time for me to go, everybody warned me that I had to be very careful with the Jim Crow laws. My brother and sister-in-law prepared my mind for what was to come. They warned me to take care of my money and to be careful in my behavior. On my arrival at the train station in Washington, D.C., I got to see life differently. The station was divided into two areas, one for the colored, one for the white. They had equal facilities as far as I could see, the room for coloreds was exactly like the one for whites, except that it was shabby and not as clean. Everywhere in the south I noticed that: the rooms for the coloreds were more neglected than those for the whites, not nearly as nice and smart or as cheerful. The same applied to the people themselves. . . .

Another incident concerning this color question occurred in Atlanta, Georgia, where I had gone to look at the work done at Spellman College. A very good friend of mine took me to a church there. She wanted me to see that they even segregated the churches. A lady missionary from South Africa talked about the work done by her mission in Africa. When the people at the church saw me, a man came out quickly and told us that we could not come into the church. "Why?" I asked. "I am a stranger here and that woman is my missionary. I am from Africa, I knew her when she was there." Of course, that was a lie, but I wanted to see for myself how the congregation would treat us. They allowed us to stay, but they refused to let us come inside the church. They found a place for us under the stairs in the vestibule. I looked at my friend and she looked at me. We only stayed there for five or ten minutes and then walked away. We just wanted the experience. . . .

My tour of the south made me think. The Jeanes system impressed me very much, but my bitterness concerning my Jim Crow experiences, made me reflect on my situation: "Why am I black? Why are brown people different? Why are whites so hostile to us?" I went to the library and started to read, searching for answers. I found many books on Sierra Leone and began to read about my own country. I read books by black authors whenever I could. Then I turned to books that dealt with the subject of white people. I read in earnest, trying to find the answers to my questions. One book that especially affected by understanding of what was going on in Africa was *How Britain Rules Africa* (1936) by George Padmore, published shortly after I returned to England. My interest in politics began to grow. . . .

Life came to a pitch when I joined the American Council for African Education (ACAE), an organization founded by Nwafor Orizu in New York City in 1944. . . .

The ACAE maintained its office at 105 Nassau Street, near Wall Street, right in the center of New York City. It had an international staff composed of whites, Africans, West Indians, and American Negroes all working in harmony. Its main objective was to promote scholarships and we gave speeches and held little conferences to further our ends. We worked arm-in-arm with the American Council on African Affairs (ACAA), the organization headed by Paul Robeson. Some of us in the ACAE were also in the executive of Robeson's group. There it was purely politics. The American authorities made trouble with Robeson because they suspected him of communist sympathies. Their suspicion also fell on those of us who associated with him. They tapped our telephones; I knew that my own phone was tapped. Whenever we called a meeting of the executive, Alphaeous Hunton, the secretary, used to come personally to inform us about it. Later, when Ghana became independent, he moved there and from there he went to Guinea. He was very helpful and kind. He visited my husband and me occasionally in Freetown.

Once I gave a talk at an ACAA meeting. I cannot remember the exact time and place, but it was on a Sunday in Brooklyn. My sister-in-law had warned me to be careful or otherwise the Americans would deport me for associating with Robeson, but I insisted on taking the risk. When I arrived at the hall, Robeson, Hunton, and the others were already there. When we began the meeting, some people in the audience, including some colored people, began to stone us with rotten eggs. We dashed back quickly without holding the meeting, and rarely did we hold a public meeting after that. The American colored people as well as the whites harassed us, but the West Indians rarely did so. I never fully comprehended the reason for this.

Remembering Robeson and Hunton and how much they helped
Africans brings Ralph Bunche to mind. Of all the Negro leaders, he
was the only one who did not cooperate with us. He was more white
than black. When he served as director of the Trusteeship Division of
the United Nations, he always refused to help us.

32

### ESLANDA GOODE ROBESON

# *We Go to Africa*

### *1936*

*Eslanda Goode Robeson (1895–1965) was a distinguished person in her
own right, besides being the wife of Paul Robeson (Document 25). Born
to an accomplished middle-class family in Washington, D.C., she won a
highly competitive scholarship to the University of Illinois, where she
majored in chemistry. She transferred to Columbia University for her
senior year, graduated in 1918, and was a pioneer African American
employee in professional positions at Presbyterian Hospital and Columbia Medical Center. At Columbia Goode met and married Paul Robeson
in 1921 while he was studying law and she was pursuing a doctorate in
anthropology. She later devoted herself to managing Paul's career and
traveled widely with him, while also lecturing and authoring three books,
including* Paul Robeson, Negro *(1930). She co-founded the Council of
African Affairs with Paul and shared with him the punishment of having
her passport withdrawn in the 1950s because of her political views. This
selection is from her account of traveling in Africa in 1936 with their
son Paul Jr. (Pauli).*

I wanted to go to Africa.

It began when I was quite small. Africa was the place we Negroes
came from originally. Lots of Americans, when they could afford it,
went back to see their "old country." I remember wanting very much
to see my "old country," and wondering what it would be like.

Eslanda Goode Robeson, *African Journey* (New York: John Day, 1945), 13–20.

Paul Robeson Jr. (left) and Eslanda Goode Robeson with Chief Justice Mula-
muzi of Uganda and an unknown boy, in Kampala, Uganda, 1936.
Reproduced with the permission of Paul Robeson Jr.

In America one heard little or nothing about Africa. I hadn't realized that, consciously, until we went to live in England. There was
rarely even a news item about Africa in American newspapers or mag-
azines. Americans were not interested in Africa economically (except
for a very few businessmen like Firestone, who has rubber interests

in Liberia), politically, or culturally. Practically nothing was or is taught in American schools about Africa. Liberia was the only place I had ever heard of, and that was because the United States maintains an American Negro consul there. Of course when I speak of Africa I mean black Africa, not North Africa.

In England, on the other hand, there is news of Africa everywhere: in the press, in the schools, in the films, in conversation. English people are actively interested in Africa economically and politically. Members of families are out in Africa in the civil service, in the military, in business; everywhere you go, someone's uncle, brother, or cousin is working, teaching, administering, or "serving" in Africa. Women go out to Africa with their men, or go out to visit them. There are courses on Africa in every good university in England; African languages are taught, missionaries are trained, and administrators are prepared for work "in the field." Everywhere there is information about Africa.

When we first went to England I remember how startled I was by all this readily available information on Africa. I had thought, somewhat complacently I'm afraid, that I was well informed about the Negro question. My grandfather, the late Francis Lewis Cardozo, was well known for his early awareness of the Negro problem, and was a pioneer in Negro education and in the fight for Negro rights. I was brought up in a household wide awake to every phase of the Negro problem in America.

There was the hitch: *in America*. There in England I was disconcerted by the fact that the Negro problem was not only the problem of the 13 million Negroes in America, but was and is the far greater problem of the 150 million Negroes in Africa, plus the problem of the 10 million Negroes in the West Indies.

Later on—much later—when I finally began to find out what it was all about, I came to realize that the Negro problem was not even limited to the problem of the 173 million black people in Africa, America, and the West Indies, but actually included (and does now especially include) the problem of the 390 million Indians in India, the problem of the 450 million Chinese in China, as well as the problem of all minorities everywhere.

It is just as well I didn't realize all this immediately. I probably would have been floored. As it was I was pretty much overcome by the fact that I knew so little concerning the problem about which I had always felt so well informed. That would never do.

I began reading everything about Africa I could lay hands on. This proved to be considerable, what with the libraries of the British Museum, the House of Commons, London University, and the London School of Economics. I began asking questions everywhere of everybody. The reading and the questions landed me right in the middle of anthropology (a subject I had only vaguely known existed) at the London School of Economics under Malinowski and Firth, and at London University under Perry and Hocart. It was all very interesting and exciting and challenging. At last I began to find out something about my "old country," my background, my people, and thus about myself.

After more than a year of very wide reading and intensive study I began to get my intellectual feet wet. I am afraid I began to be obstreperous in seminars. I soon became fed up with white students and teachers "interpreting" the Negro mind and character to me. Especially when I felt, as I did very often, that their interpretation was wrong.

It went something like this: Me, I *am* Negro, I *know* what we think, how we feel. I know this means that, and that means so-and-so.

"Ah, no, my dear, you're wrong. You see, you are European.* You can't possibly know how the primitive mind works until you study it, as we have done."

"What do you mean I'm European? I'm *Negro*. I'm African myself. I'm what you call primitive. I have studied my mind, our minds. How dare you call me European!"

"No, you're not primitive, my dear," they told me patiently, tolerantly, "you're educated and cultured, like us."

"I'm educated because I went to school, because I was taught. You're educated because you went to school, were taught. I'm cultured because my people had the education and the means to achieve a good standard of living; that's the reason you're cultured. 'Poor whites' have neither education nor culture. Africans would have both if they had the schools and the money. Going to school and having money doesn't make me European. Having no schools and no money doesn't make the African primitive." I protested furiously.

"No, no," they explained; "the primitive mind cannot grasp the kind of ideas we can; they have schools, but their schools have only simple

*"European," a term which is very widely and somewhat loosely used among anthropologists, usually means "white," not only in color, but in culture, in civilization; "European" in their usage generally means a white person with Western (as against oriental and primitive) education, background, and values.

subjects, and crafts; it's all very different. You see, we've been out there for years and years (some ten, some twenty, some thirty years); we've studied them, taught them, administered them, worked with them, and we know. You've never been out there, you've never seen them and talked with them on their home ground; you can't possibly know."

It all sounded nonsense to me. And yet the last bit made sense — maybe. I'd better check it. Paul and I began to seek out all the Africans we could find, everywhere we went: in England, Scotland, Ireland, France; in the universities, on the docks, in the slums. The more we talked with them, the more we came to know them, the more convinced we were that we are the same people: They know us, we know them; we understand their spoken and unspoken word, we have the same kind of ideas, the same ambitions, the same kind of humor, many of the same values.

I asked Africans I met at universities, taking honors in medicine, in law, in philosophy, in education, in other subjects: "What is all this about primitive minds and abstruse subjects, about only simple subjects and crafts in your schools?"

"Oh, *that*," they said with a twinkle, "there's nothing primitive about our minds in these universities, is there? And how can we cope with any but simple subjects and crafts in our schools, when that is all they will allow us to have? Actually, they rarely give us any schools at all, but they sometimes 'aid' the schools the Missions have set up for us, and those we have set up for ourselves with our own money and labor. But they definitely limit our curricula."

I began to see light. It was the old army game every Negro in America will recognize: The white American South says the Negro is ignorant, and has a low standard of living; the Negro says the South won't give him adequate schools or decent wages.

With new confidence I began to ask more questions in seminars. And always I came up against the blank wall: "But I was out there thirty years — I know. You have never been out there — you simply don't know."

"I *am* one, so I know."

And they would say: "You're different; you've met a few European-educated Africans who are different too."

This pattern was familiar to me also. In America Negroes get the same reaction: White America generalizes in its mind about the primitiveness, ignorance, laziness, and smell of Negroes. When we protest that these descriptions are just not true of us, nor of millions of our fellow Negroes, they answer: "But you are different; you are the exceptions." No matter how many facts we marshal to prove their statements untrue, they close their minds against these facts. It is more convenient for them to believe their own generalizations than to face the facts. So the facts become the "exceptions." But we "special" Negroes look closely and thoughtfully at the facts. We know we aren't essentially different from our fellow Negroes. We know also that others' merely saying we are different does not make us so.

So far, so good. But I had no answer to the constant "You have never been out there." Very well, I would go. I'd just have to go out to Africa and see and meet and study and talk with my people on their home ground. Then I would be able to say truly: I have been there too, and I *know*.

Paul couldn't go to Africa with me. He had contracts ahead for two years and couldn't risk not being able to fulfill them. We knew nothing, firsthand, about climate and conditions in Africa. Paul doesn't stand the heat well, changes of climate are hard on him, changes of diet and water put him off. Perhaps it was best for me to go first, find out as much as I could about everything, and next time we could go together.

And so we began to plan: While I was away, Mother could go to Russia to visit my two brothers who live and work there. Paul would go to Russia later on and spend some time with Sergei Eisenstein, who was making a film in the country outside Moscow. The idea of Paul making a Russian film had been discussed; this would give him a chance to perfect his Russian and observe Soviet methods of film making.

That disposed of everybody but Pauli, our beloved only child. He was eight—a fairly tender age; he was sturdy, but Mamma had always most carefully supervised his diet and general regime, which was rather strict. But he was adventurous, like me.

What was more important, Paul and I remembered vividly the time when, on the set of the *Sanders of the River* film, Pauli had been astonished and delighted to see all the Africans. "Why, there are lots of brown people," this then six-year-old had said happily, "lots of black people too; we're not the only ones." We had been profoundly disturbed by the realization that he had been living in an entirely white world since we had brought him and my mother to live with us in England, when he was ten months old. The only Negroes he had seen besides ourselves and Larry (Lawrence Brown, our colleague and accompanist) were the occasional ones who visited at our home. His young mind had thought we were the only brown people in a totally white world.

We must do something about that, we had said then. Well, this is it; this is what we'll do. If some Africans on a film set open up a new world to the child, a trip to the heart of Africa itself will be a revelation. He will see millions of other brown and black people, he will see a black world, he will see a black continent. So it was decided that Pauli would go with me.

We made our plans: We would go by sea from England to Capetown and Port Elizabeth, right at the bottom of South Africa. We would try to connect up with Bokwe, our African friend who had finished medicine at Edinburgh University and gone home to Alice, Cape Province, to practice; and his sister Frieda and her husband Zach Matthews, whom we had known in London when he was attending the Malinowski seminars; they and their children also lived at Alice, where Matthews was teaching at Fort Hare, the African college. Then we would go on to Johannesburg and maybe see the mines; and perhaps work in a trip to Swaziland; and maybe I could manage to run up to see Tshekedi Khama, the African regent we had all been so thrilled about. Then we would go down to Mozambique in Portuguese East Africa, pick up a ship and sail up the east coast to Mombasa, and go overland by train to join Nyabongo, an African student of anthropology at Oxford, who would be at home in Uganda for the summer. It was arranged that Nyabongo would meet us at Kampala and take us out to his home in Toro, where I planned to do my fieldwork on the herdspeople. Then we would fly home from Entebbe. All very ambitious.

We got down to brass tacks. There were vaccinations and injections to be taken at the Hospital for Tropical Diseases. There was shopping to do: tropical clothes, mosquito boots, cholera belts for Pauli and me; tropical luggage; my Cine-kodak to check, and a lot of films especially packed for the tropics to buy. Paul gave me a gem of a camera, a Rolleiflex. "You can't take too many pictures," he said wisely. There were ship and rail reservations, passports to be put in order, visits to the Colonial Office, and visas.

The visas were the real problem. It seems if you are Negro, you can't make up your mind to go to Africa, and just go. Oh, no. Not unless you are a missionary. The white people in Africa do not want educated Negroes traveling around seeing how their brothers live; nor do they want those brothers seeing Negroes from other parts of the world, hearing how they live. It would upset them, make them restless and dissatisfied; it would make them examine and re-examine the conditions under which they, as "natives," live; and that would never do at all, at all. In fact it would be extremely dangerous. Something must be done to prevent this "contact." But what to do? It's simple: just keep all other Negroes out of Africa, except maybe a few who will come to preach the Gospel. The Gospel always helps to keep people quiet and resigned. And how to keep them out? That's simple, too: just don't grant them visas. So they don't grant them visas. *Voilà*.

I had had a fair amount of experience traveling about with Paul and Larry all over Europe and to Russia. On concert tours I always took care of tickets, passports, itinerary, foreign monies for us all. For this trip I planned a rather elastic itinerary, bought steamer reservations at Cooks', hied me to the Colonial Office for visas to Swaziland, Basutoland, Kenya, Uganda, Egypt (for the air trip home).

The Colonial Office wanted to know why I was going. I was going out to do my fieldwork for a degree in anthropology. When I presented my credentials from the professors at school the Colonial Office was helpful and gave me all the visas.

Then to South Africa House, but no South African visa.

"Why not?" I asked innocently. Well, it seems all visas are granted from the home office in Capetown, and mails take time. "All right, it takes time. I have time; I'll come back."

Our arms swelled up and became stiff and sore from the vaccinations and injections. Our luggage accumulated, and the time for sailing drew near. Back to South Africa House—still no visas.

"Still no word," they said.

"I'll gladly pay for cables, to hurry it up," I said.

A few days more, and still no word.

"I'll gladly pay for telephone calls through to the Capetown office," I said.

Another few days, and still no visa.

Then Paul and I took counsel.

"They're not going to give us visas," I said. "I recognize the runaround in this 'still no word' business."

We were angry, frustrated.

I said, "They will have to tell me no, and why, before I give up."

"So they will tell you no," said Paul, "and then you can't go."

"But I've got to go," I said. "Pauli and I will just get on that ship, with or without visas. When we get there, all they can do is to refuse to let us land. If they do that, I'll set up a howl there, and you can set up a real howl here, and then maybe they'll do something."

"It sounds crazy," said Paul, "just crazy enough to work. The worst that can happen is that you'll miss South Africa and have to go right on up the east coast without stopping off."

Cooks' said I couldn't sail without visas. It just wasn't done.

"But we've got visas," I said, waving our passports. "Swaziland, Basutoland, Bechuanaland, Kenya, Uganda, Egypt."

"Well——" said Cooks'.

"Well," I said firmly, "we'll go, and if necessary we'll just have to miss South Africa."

So we set out. On May 29, 1936, Pauli and I took the boat train from London to Southampton, for the steamship *Winchester Castle*, of the Union Castle Line. We bade good-by to Mother at the flat. Paul took us to Waterloo Station and settled us in the train. Larry came to see us off.

Paul said, as he kissed us good-by: "I'll stay right here in London near the telephone till you are well on your way at the other end, and this visa business has been cleared up."

He is such a dear person. It was a wrench to leave him. He and Pauli had spent all the day before at Lords', sitting on the bleachers in the sun holding hands, watching a cricket match. Pauli found it hard to leave him too. But we had each other, and we were off on high adventure. We sat close together and held hands all the way to Southampton.

<br>

33

### ERA BELL THOMPSON

## An African American in Africa

### 1953

---

*A childhood in Iowa and North Dakota is an unusual background for a successful African American journalist, but Era Bell Thompson (1905–1986) was an unusual woman. With a new bachelor's degree in journalism from an Iowa college, she headed for Chicago, where she soon at-*

---

Era Bell Thompson, *Africa, Land of My Fathers* (Garden City, N.Y.: Doubleday, 1954), 16–17, 43, 52–53, 62, 64, 280–81.

*tracted attention for her critical writing on Marcus Garvey. Her political views remained moderate during the following turbulent decades, but her reporting was always insightful and factual. In 1945 she won a prestigious Newberry Fellowship, which permitted her to complete her autobiography,* American Daughter *(1946). She wrote for* Negro Digest *and then the new* Ebony *magazine, of which she was co-managing editor from 1951 to 1964. It was in that capacity that she made the tour of Africa that is the subject of this selection.*

Until a few months before, Africa had been the last place on earth I wanted to visit. Until a few years before, my knowledge of the continent, like that of most Americans, both black and white, was geared to concepts handed down by Livingstone and Stanley nearly a hundred years ago. And like most American Negroes, I was so busy shedding my African heritage and fighting for my rights as an American citizen that what happened to my 175,000,000 brothers beyond the sea was a matter for the missionaries. Had anyone called me an African I would have been indignant. Only race fanatics flaunted their jungle ancestry or formed back-to-Africa movements—and they were usually motivated more by a king complex than by any loyalty to black genes.

When I saw bare-toed African students walking down Chicago boulevards in their flowing robes and colorful head cloths, I, too, shook my head and murmured, "My people!" If there was the skeleton of a chief in my family closet, he was Cherokee, not Kru; Black Foot, not Yoruba or Fulani. I was proud only of my red and white blood, ashamed of the black, for I grew up believing that black was bad, that black was dirty and poor and wrong. Black was Africa. I did not want to be an African. . . .

Little by little I heard and read about another Africa, one that went beyond ignorance and savagery, an Africa pieced together by black historians from facts disregarded by white historians who said Africa had no past, its people no culture. I learned that in the now Anglo-Egyptian Sudan a Negro empire flourished five thousand years before the birth of Christ. In the Middle Ages, Africa had a civilization in the West that even antedated that of Europe, and my heathen progenitors were working with wood and metal, molding pottery, weaving cloth, and creating an alphabet while European Nordics were still carrying stone clubs.

The word "black" became less repulsive as knowledge of my forebears increased, the word "African" became less embarrassing as I became aware of the true story of Africa's rich contributions to mankind; yet the world clung tenaciously to its picture of Congo swamps and voodoo incantations.

I tried to put Africa out of my mind, but it kept cropping up in the news. After World War II, the spotlight of world attention shifted to the great continent and its rich resources. With the loss of its Asian colonies, Europe was looking to the gold, diamonds, and uranium in "them thar" African hills. America was also looking toward Africa for new land, air bases, and strategic raw materials. The African himself was demanding to be heard, and the same wave of nationalism that set brown Asia free was knocking on black Africa's door.

Out of the West came a dark Moses named Kwame Nkrumah, who, as Prime Minister of the Gold Coast, was demanding an end to colonialism. In the East, Mau Mau terrorists were bent on a crusade to rid their land of its white settlers. In the North the long pent-up feelings of the Moroccans flared anew and French blood was spilled in the streets of Casablanca. In the Union of South Africa Dr. Malan's system of *apartheid* was fanning the hatred of black men and brown.

Africa moved into the headlines. Big-time newspaper and magazine correspondents, trekking through the bush, soon outnumbered anthropologists and men of God, for there was a sudden urgency to shed new light on the Dark Continent.

Along with a few million other American Negroes, I began to take new interest and a growing pride in the Motherland. If my heathen relatives were about to reinherit their fathers' kingdoms, I would be among the first to congratulate them. It would be interesting to see what would happen if I went "home." Would the folks welcome me back after three hundred years? And how would I feel about them? . . .

My magazine wanted me to go to Ife and see how the descendants of the West African Adam and Eve were making out. Nigeria is also said to be the chief country from which my own forebears came. Despite heavy and repeated raids by slave traders between the sixteenth and nineteenth centuries, it was still the most populous (thirty million) country in Africa. Nigeria was more "home" to me than Liberia, whose founders were merely transplanted American Negroes whose ancestors originally came from Nigeria and other coastal countries. More important than either the legend or my exact lineage was the fact that archaeologists in Ife were still turning up evidences of that ancient African culture that had so bolstered my racial pride. . . .

By mid-morning we reached the outskirts of Ife, the Garden of Eden, Sacred City of the Yorubas. Stretched out before us was a long, winding street, lined with brown mud shacks. Clothing which hung on bamboo poles outside of tiny shops was soiled and rain-stained; bolts of cloth lay on makeshift shelves; tinware hung precariously in doorways. The nude babies of women shopkeepers broke from their nursing to play in the street among the goats and chickens. Farther back, behind the low huts, were the square pastel homes of wealthy cocoa farmers and merchants.

This, then, was Paradise! This was where Odudua descended from heaven in the beginning—or came down from Egypt early in the twelfth century, as some believe.

We drove directly to the colonnaded Council Hall where court was in session. Sitting on his dais was the portly Oni of Ife, dressed in a white-and-gray-striped cloth with matching turban. Around him sat the councilors and judges. Before the court in box stalls stood the plaintiff and defendant. Guards led us to the rear of the court to a small anteroom. In a few minutes the Oni himself, Sir Adesoji Aderemi, K.B.E., C.M.G., and Minister without Portfolio, came out smiling. I liked him immediately. He looked for all the world like a Chicago baritone ready to run through a dress rehearsal of *The Hot Mikado*.

"Later, I will talk with you," he said, more like an American than an English subject. "If I adjourn court now, we'll never settle this case." With that, the spiritual leader of six and a half million Yorubas smiled pleasantly, bowed, and returned to his court.

Outside of the hall we were joined by Bernard Fagg, a European archaeologist employed by the Antiquity Service of the Nigerian Government to install all existing Ife art in the new museum, to restore other treasures in their present settings, and to dig up anything else that might add to the city's illustrious past. Fagg took us to a fresh excavation, site of an ancient shrine, only a few feet from the Council Hall and showed us one of his prize discoveries, the Iron of Ladi.

Now, Ladi was a famous blacksmith and he, like all Yoruba gods of long ago, was a regular John Henry. How long ago depended on which school of Ife legend one believed. According to the Garden theory, Ladi was one of the Originals. According to the down-from-Egypt version, the boy would still be pre-twelfth century. His iron hammer weighed two hundred pounds; his stone anvil, its base still buried in ancient ground, had not been lifted by twentieth-century hands. Ladi's anvil was now used for oath-taking, they reluctantly told me, a cere-mony which consisted of drinking palm wine mixed with the blood of a dead pigeon.

At the excavation a well-shaped granite fish had also been found, and several feet farther down were evidences of paved streets, built at the direction of the tyrannical Oluwo, Ife's only female oni, paved streets that belonged to that early African civilization the existence of which many present-day historians deny. . . .

But what did Nigerians think of the American Negro? Those who had lived in America liked us, but they did not always understand our ways.

"We have always believed that all black people are brothers," a busi-nessman told me. "If you are colored, the African says that you must be taken care of. American Negroes do not feel that way. If an African goes to them for help, they feel no obligation to him."

"We do not expect you to renounce your American citizenship," said another man. "You are American by birth, but racially we are brothers."

Said a Nigerian woman, wife of a student in America, "There are as yet no strong ties between Nigeria and America, although one can notice the beginning."

Then they told me a story. Not long before I arrived, an American Negro visited Nigeria and the red carpet was rolled out. Wined and dined was this person, and showered with gifts and given two thou-sand dollars in cash. Back in America, the ungrateful one told the press that Nigerians were barbarians. That did it. Free transportation and accommodations, they said, were no longer offered to American Negro visitors.

I did not know the person who had done them wrong, but I do know the mysterious ways in which the press sometimes works and how easy it is to be misquoted or quoted out of context. I also know how different it is to retract or correct a statement once it has been printed. I was not defending the ungrateful one, but I was disappointed to think that blacks, of all people, should judge a whole nationality by the behavior of one of its members. . . .

The plane back to Accra was another cargo ship, but a vast improve-ment over the first one. It had air vents and covers on the backs of the seats. It also had both African and European passengers. I was curious about the way we would be seated. . . .

The pilot began to seat the passengers. All of the Africans were taken up front. In the four-chaired back compartment, he placed the four whites. I was put in the last seat rear of the forward compartment, all by myself. . . .

Yes, I had traversed the length and breadth of Africa, seeking a bond between the American Negro and his African brother; but the African, I found, knows even less about us than we do about him. And small wonder.

Some three hundred years ago we sailed away in slave ships and few of us have returned. Until World War II, when some of our G.I.s were stationed there, and Africans were sent abroad to fight, few Africans had ever seen a real live American Negro. Even in English-speaking countries, practically no news of us seeps through to their world. In the Union of South Africa, Negro publications—and Negroes—are barred. Few American Negroes travel as far as Africa, and when they do, their destination is usually the west coast. The only Negroes who have the means and the inclination to venture farther into the interior are missionaries (and in many sections they are now barred), an occasional State Department representative on a prescribed tour, or a research student looking for the same primitiveness white research students are looking for.

But to those Africans who do have knowledge of us, the bond is real—the blood thick. Come home, they say, all is forgiven. We need your skill and your capital to help us develop the land that we have and to regain the land that has been taken from us.

And how do I feel, now, about them?

I am proud of the African blood in my veins and proud of my black heritage, for I have seen evidences of that ancient African civilization in the excavations of Ife, and I have talked with black kings who are the descendants of African conquerors, and I have walked in the streets of a black kingdom whose Christianity is among the oldest in the world.

Africans are my brothers, for we are of one race. But Africa, the land of my fathers, is not my home.

I am an American—an American by nationality, a citizen of the United States by birth. I owe my loyalty and my allegiance to but one flag. I have but one country.

# 34

## MAYA ANGELOU

# *An African American in Ghana*

### *1963*

---

*Born Marguerite Johnson in St. Louis in 1928, Maya Angelou is better known by her professional name as a poet, playwright, author, documentary producer, and activist. A civil rights activist, she was the northern coordinator of the Southern Christian Leadership Conference. She became internationally known after the publication of her autobiographical* I Know Why the Caged Bird Sings *(1970), written after her return from five years in Africa. The book stayed on the* New York Times *best-selling book list for two years—a record for a nonfiction work by a black writer. Her hard-earned fame has brought her many awards, including nominations for the Pulitzer Prize and the National Book Award and membership on two presidential commissions. Since 1981 she has been a professor of American Studies at Wake Forest University. This selection is from her fifth book, describing some of her impressions of post-independence Ghana, where she was feature editor of the* African Review *and taught at the University of Ghana.*

---

The community of Black immigrants opened and fitted me into their lives as if they had been saving my place.

The group's leader, if such a collection of eccentric egos could be led, was Julian. He had three books published in the United States, had acted in a Broadway play, and was a respected American-based intellectual before an encounter with the CIA and the FBI caused him to flee his country for Africa. He was accompanied in flight and supported, in fact, by Ana Livia, who was at least as politically volatile as he.

Sylvia Boone, a young sociologist, had come to Africa first on a church affiliated tour, then returned with sophistication, a second Master's degree, and fluent French to find her place on the Continent.

---

Maya Angelou, *All God's Children Need Traveling Shoes* (New York: Random House, 1986), 18–21.

Ted Pointiflet was a painter who argued gently, but persistently that Africa was the inevitable destination of all Black Americans. Lesley Lacy, a sleek graduate student, was an expert on Marxism and Garveyism, while Jim and Annette Lacy, no relation to Lesley, were grade school teachers and quite rare among our group because they listened more than they talked. The somber faced Frank Robinson, a plumber, had a contagious laughter, and a fierce devotion to Nkrumah. Vicki Garvin had been a union organizer, Alice Windom had been trained in sociology. I called the group "Revolutionist Returnees."

Each person had brought to Africa varying talents, energies, vigor, youth, and terrible yearnings to be accepted. On Julian's side porch during warm black nights, our voices were raised in attempts to best each other in lambasting America and extolling Africa.

We drank gin and ginger ale when we could afford it, and Club beer when our money was short. We did not discuss the open gutters along the streets of Accra, the shacks of corrugated iron in certain neighborhoods, dirty beaches, and voracious mosquitoes. And under no circumstances did we mention our disillusionment at being overlooked by the Ghanaians.

We had come home, and if home was not what we had expected, never mind, our need for belonging allowed us to ignore the obvious and to create real places or even illusory places, befitting our imagination.

Doctors were in demand, so Ana Livia had been quickly placed in the Military Hospital and within a year, had set up a woman's clinic where she and her platoon of nursing sisters treated up to two hundred women daily. Progressive journalists were sought after, so Julian, who wrote articles for American and African journals, also worked for the *Ghana Evening News*. Frank and his partner Carlos Allston from Los Angeles founded a plumbing and electric company. Their success gave heart to the rest. We had little doubt about our likability. After the Africans got to know us their liking would swiftly follow. We didn't question if we would be useful. Our people for over three hundred years had been made so useful, a bloody war had been fought and lost, rather than have our usefulness brought to an end. Since we were descendants of African slaves torn from the land, we reasoned we wouldn't have to earn the right to return, yet we wouldn't be so arrogant as to take anything for granted. We would work and produce, then snuggle down into Africa as a baby nuzzles in a mother's arms.

I was soon swept into an adoration for Ghana as a young girl falls in love, heedless and with slight chance of finding the emotion requited.

There was an obvious justification for my amorous feelings. Our people had always longed for home. For centuries we had sung about a place not built with hands, where the streets were paved with gold, and were washed with honey and milk. There the saints would march around wearing white robes and jeweled crowns. There, at last, we would study war no more and, more important, no one would wage war against us again.

The old Black deacons, ushers, mothers of the church, and junior choirs only partially meant heaven as that desired destination. In the yearning, heaven and Africa were inextricably combined.

And now, less than one hundred years after slavery was abolished, some descendants of those early slaves taken from Africa, returned, weighted with a heavy hope, to a continent which they could not remember, to a home which had shamefully little memory of them.

Which one of us could know that years of bondage, brutalities, the mixture of other bloods, customs, and languages had transformed us into an unrecognizable tribe? Of course, we knew that we were mostly unwanted in the land of our birth and saw promise on our ancestral continent.

I was in Ghana by accident, literally, but the other immigrants had chosen the country because of its progressive posture and its brilliant president, Kwame Nkrumah. He had let it be known that American Negroes would be welcome to Ghana. He offered havens for Southern and East African revolutionaries working to end colonialism in their countries.

I admitted that while Ghana's domestic and foreign policy were stimulating, I was captured by the Ghanaian people. Their skins were the colors of my childhood cravings: peanut butter, licorice, chocolate, and caramel. Theirs was the laughter of home, quick and without artifice. The erect and graceful walk of the women reminded me of my Arkansas grandmother, Sunday-hatted, on her way to church. I listened to men talk, and whether or not I understood their meaning, there was a melody as familiar as sweet potato pie, reminding me of my Uncle Tommy Baxter in Santa Monica, California. So I had finally come home. The prodigal child, having strayed, been stolen or sold from the land of her fathers, having squandered her mother's gifts, and having laid down in cruel gutters, had at last arisen and directed herself back to the welcoming arms of the family where she would be bathed, clothed with fine raiment, and seated at the welcoming table.

I was one of nearly two hundred Black Americans from St. Louis, New York City, Washington, D.C., Los Angeles, Atlanta, and Dallas who hoped to live out the Biblical story.

Some travelers had arrived at Ghana's Accra Airport, expecting customs agents to embrace them, porters to shout—"welcome," and the taxi drivers to ferry them, horns blaring, to the city square where smiling officials would cover them in ribbons and clasp them to their breasts with tearful sincerity. Our arrival had little impact on anyone but us. We ogled the Ghanaians and few of them even noticed. The newcomers hid disappointment in quick repartee, in jokes and clenched jaws.

The citizens were engaged in their own concerns. They were busy adoring their flag, their five-year-old independence from Britain, and their president.

# A Chronology of Events in the Black Atlantic (1770–1965)

**1772** Somerset Decision rules that slavery is not recognized in British law.

**1773** Phillis Wheatley arrives in Great Britain, where the countess of Huntington arranges to publish a book of her poetry.

**1787** The Province of Freedom is founded in Sierra Leone.

**1789** Olaudah Equiano (Gustavus Vassa) publishes the first edition of his autobiography in London.

**1792** Thomas Peters and other black Loyalists settle in Sierra Leone.

**1808** Transatlantic slave trade becomes illegal for British subjects; navy patrol is headquartered in Sierra Leone.

**1815** Paul Cuffe of Massachusetts settles thirty-eight free American blacks in Sierra Leone.

**1821** Liberia is founded by the American Colonization Society as an African settlement colony.

**1834** Slaves are emancipated in British colonies.

**1847** Liberia becomes an independent republic under Americo-Liberian rule.

**1850** Fugitive Slave Law passed in the United States.

**1859** Martin Delany explores the Niger in search of a home for African Americans.

**1862** Edward W. Blyden is appointed professor of classics at Liberia College.

**1864** Samuel Ajayi Crowther is consecrated an Anglican bishop for the lower Niger River.

**1865** Thirteenth Amendment to the Constitution frees slaves in the United States.

**1868**  James A. B. Horton, M.D., publishes *West African Countries and Peoples*, advocating more Liberia-style nations in West Africa.

**1875**  Emma White settles in Opobo to work for Jaja.

**1881**  Booker T. Washington founds Tuskegee Institute.

**1890**  George Washington Williams petitions President Benjamin Harrison over the Congo Free State.

**1893**  American Missionary Association sponsors World Congress on Africa.

**1898**  African Methodist Episcopal bishop Henry McNeal Turner makes official visit to southern Africa.

**1900**  First Pan-African Congress is held in London.

**1914**  Marcus Garvey founds the Universal Negro Improvement Association (UNIA) in Jamaica.

**1914**  James Aggrey arrives in New York City from the Gold Coast Colony to study at Columbia University.

**1915**  Rev. John Chilembwe leads revolt for black equality in colonial Nyasaland.

**1920**  UNIA convention in New York City elects Marcus Garvey the provisional president of Africa.

**1921**  Second Pan-African Congress meets in London.

**1923**  Third Pan-African Congress meets in London.

**1925**  Benjamin Nnamdi Azikiwe arrives in the United States to study, remaining until 1934.

**1927**  Fourth Pan-African Congress meets in New York City.

**1927**  Marcus Garvey deported from the United States after serving two years in prison for embezzlement.

**1936**  Constance Horton arrives in the United States from Sierra Leone for study.

**1936**  Eslanda Goode Robeson travels to South Africa with Paul Robeson Jr.

**1936**  Emperor Haile Selassie pleads unsuccessfully for the League of Nations to save Ethiopia from Italian conquest.

**1937**  Paul Robeson and Max Yergen found the Council on African Affairs.

**1937**  International African Service Bureau is founded in London.

**1939**  Aimé Césaire publishes his poem "Cahier d'un retour au pays natal."

**1945** Fifth Pan-African Congress meets in Manchester (U.K.).

**1947** W. E. B. Du Bois publishes *The World and Africa.*

**1953** Era Bell Thompson tours Africa.

**1957** Kwame Nkrumah leads Ghana to independence.

**1960** Nnamdi Azikiwe leads Nigeria to independence; Léopold Senghor leads Senegal to independence.

**1963** Maya Angelou begins an extended residence in Ghana.

# Questions for Consideration

1. What were the advantages and problems of blacks' moving to Africa in the eighteenth and nineteenth centuries?
2. How did African Americans view the role of Christianity in improving African lives? Did Africans see things differently?
3. How did black attitudes toward the colonization of Africa change over time?
4. Which authors saw black commonality as based on biology (race), on culture, or on discrimination by whites?
5. What different strategies were advocated for freeing diaspora blacks from racial discrimination?
6. What strategies did Africans use to free themselves from white rule?
7. Assess the importance of Marcus Garvey and the UNIA.
8. Why was black unity such an important issue in the twentieth century?
9. Assess the importance of West Indians in the Pan-Africanist movement.
10. Why did W. E. B. Du Bois attach special significance to his meeting the president of Liberia?
11. Do you agree with Kwame Nkrumah's assessment that the first four Pan-African Congresses were "rather nebulous"?
12. In the twentieth century how did the reasons African Americans went to Africa differ from the reasons Africans went to the United States?
13. What role did the Communist party play in black struggles in the twentieth century?
14. Paul Robeson spoke of blacks joining a "world-community"; Léopold Senghor spoke of Universal Civilization. How similar are these ideas, and can you find other authors in the documents who adhered to similar ideas?

# Selected Bibliography

GENERAL WORKS

Campbell, James. *Middle Passages: African American Journeys to Africa, 1787–2005.* New York: Penguin, 2006.

Conyers, James L. Jr., ed. *Black Lives: Essays in African American Biography.* Armonk, N.Y.: M. E. Sharpe, 1999. [Aggrey and Turner]

Esedebe, P. Olisanwuche. *Pan-Africanism: The Idea and the Movement, 1776–1991.* 2nd ed. Washington, D.C.: Howard University Press, 1994.

Fryer, Peter. *Staying Power: The History of Black People in Britain.* London and Boulder: Pluto Press, 1984.

Gates, Henry Louis, Jr., and William L. Andrews, eds. *Pioneers of the Black Atlantic: Five Slave Narratives from the Enlightenment, 1772–1815.* Washington, D.C.: Counterpoint, 1998.

Gerzina, Gretchen. *Black London: Life before Emancipation.* New Brunswick, N.J.: Rutgers University Press, 1995.

Gilroy, Paul. *The Black Atlantic: Modernity and Double-Consciousness.* Cambridge, Mass.: Harvard University Press, 1995.

Gomez, Michael. *A History of the African Diaspora.* New York: Cambridge University Press, 2005.

Kilson, Martin, and Adelaide Hill, eds. *Apropos of Africa: Afro-American Leaders and the Romance of Africa.* Garden City, N.Y.: Doubleday, 1971.

Kopytoff, Jean Herskovits. *A Preface to Modern Nigeria: The "Sierra Leonians" in Yoruba, 1830–1890.* Madison: University of Wisconsin Press, 1965.

Lipschutz, Mark R., and R. Kent Rasmussen. *Dictionary of African Historical Biography.* 2nd ed. Berkeley: University of California Press, 1987.

Lynch, Hollis R. "Pan-Negro Nationalism in the New World, before 1862." In *Boston University Papers on Africa,* vol. 2, edited by Jeffrey Butler, 147–79. Boston: Boston University Press, 1966.

Meriwether, James H. *Proudly We Can Be Africans: Black Americans and Africa, 1935–1961.* Chapel Hill: University of North Carolina Press, 2002.

Richardson, Alan, and Debbie Lee, eds. *Early Black British Writing: Olaudah Equiano, Mary Prince, and Others.* Boston: Houghton Mifflin, 2004.

Sanneh, Lamin. *Abolitionists Abroad: American Blacks and the Making of Modern West Africa*. Cambridge, Mass.: Harvard University Press, 1999.

Schama, Simon. *Rough Crossings: Britain, the Slaves, and the American Revolution*. London: BBC Books, 2005.

Segal, Ronald. *The Black Diaspora: Five Centuries of the Black Experience outside Africa*. New York: Farrar, Straus and Giroux, 1995.

Sundiata, Ibrahim. *Brothers and Strangers: Black Zion, Black Slavery, 1914–1940*. Durham, N.C.: Duke University Press, 2003.

Williams, Walter L. *Black Americans and the Evangelization of Africa, 1877–1900*. Madison: University of Wisconsin Press, 1982.

INDIVIDUAL LIVES AND TEXTS

Angelou, Maya. *All God's Children Need Traveling Shoes*. New York: Random House, 1986.

Azikiwe, Nnamdi. *My Odyssey: An Autobiography*. New York: Praeger Publishers, 1970.

Blyden, Edward W. *Christianity, Islam, and the Negro Race*. 2nd ed. London: W. B. Whittingham, 1888.

Cronon, E. David. *Marcus Garvey and the Universal Negro Improvement Association*. Madison: University of Wisconsin Press, 1969.

Cummings-John, Constance Agatha. *Memoirs of a Krio Leader*. Edited by LaRay Denzer. Ibadan, Nigeria: Sam Bookman for Humanities Research Center, 1995.

Delany, Martin R. *The Condition, Elevation, Emigration, and Destiny of the Colored People of the United States* and *Official Report of the Niger Valley Exploring Party*. With an introduction by Toyin Falola. Amherst, N.Y.: Humanity Books, 2004.

Douglass, Frederick. *Narrative of the Life of Frederick Douglass, an American Slave, Written by Himself.* Edited by David W. Blight. Boston: Bedford Books, 1993.

Equiano, Olaudah. *The Interesting Life of Olaudah Equiano, Written by Himself.* 2nd ed. Edited by Robert J. Allison. Boston: Bedford/St. Martin's, 2007.

Franklin, John Hope. *George Washington Williams: A Biography*. Chicago: University of Chicago Press, 1985.

Fyfe, Christopher. *Africanus Horton: West African Scientist and Patriot, 1835–1883*. New York: Oxford University Press, 1972.

Kennedy, Pagan. *Black Livingstone: A True Tale of Adventure in the Nineteenth-Century Congo*. New York: Viking, 2002. [William Henry Sheppard]

Lynch, Hollis R. *Edward Wilmot Blyden: Pan-Negro Patriot, 1832–1912*. London: Oxford University Press, 1967.

McFeely, William S. *Frederick Douglass*. New York: Simon & Schuster, 1991.

Nkrumah, Kwame. *Ghana: The Autobiography of Kwame Nkrumah.* New York: International Publishers, 1971.

Phipps, William E. *William Sheppard: Congo's African American Livingstone.* Louisville, Ky.: Geneva Press, 2002.

Smith, Edwin W. *Aggrey of Africa: A Study in Black and White.* New York: For the Phelps-Stokes Fund by the Friendship Press, 1929.

Thompson, Era Bell. *Africa, Land of My Fathers.* Garden City, N.Y.: Doubleday, 1954.

Ullman, Victor. *Martin R. Delany: The Beginnings of Black Nationalism.* Boston: Beacon Press, 1971.

Wamba, Philippe. *Kinship: A Family's Journey in Africa and America.* New York: Penguin Books, 2000.

Wheatley, Phillis. *Complete Writings.* Edited by Vincent Carretta. New York: Penguin Books, 2001.

# ACKNOWLEDGMENTS

**Document 20:** Reproduced with permission of Curtis Brown Group Ltd, London on behalf of the Estate of C. L. R. James. Copyright © C. L. R. James 1963.

**Document 21:** Kwame Nkrumah, *Africa Must Unite.* © 1963 Kwame Nkrumah. © 1971 International Publishers. Co., Inc. Used with the kind permission of International Publishers Co., Inc.

**Document 23:** Ralph J. Bunche, "Some Reflections on Peace in Our Times." © The Nobel Foundation 1950. Used by permission of the Nobel Foundation.

**Documents 25 and 32:** Paul Robeson, "I Want to Be an African." © 1934, and Eslanda Goode Robeson, *African Journey*, pp. 13–20. © 1945. Used by permission of Paul Robeson Jr.

**Document 28:** Léopold Sêdar Senghor, "Négritude et la civilization de l'universel," *Liberté III.* © Éditions du Seuil, 1977. Translated with the permission of Éditions du Seuil, Paris.

**Document 30:** Nnamdi Azikiwe, *My Odyssey: An Autobiography.* © 1970 by Praeger Publishers. Reproduced with permission of Greenwood Publishing Group, Inc., Westport, Conn.

**Document 31:** Constance Cummings-John, *Memoirs of a Krio Leader.* © 1995 by Constance Agatha Cummings-John. Reproduced with the kind permission of LaRay Denzer, editor.

**Document 33:** From *Africa, Land of My Fathers* by Era Bell Thompson, copyright 1954 by Era Bell Thompson. Used by permission of Doubleday, a division of Random House, Inc.

**Document 35:** From *All God's Children Need Traveling Shoes* by Maya Angelou, copyright 1986 by Maya Angelou. Used by permission of Random House, Inc.

# Index

**175**